PRAISE FOR THAT'S MY GOD

I have known Cindi Lombardo for well over twenty-five years. I have seen her move people to Christ time and time again. *That's My God* continues her ministry and is a must-read for Christians and all people of faith. It is the definition of amazing grace!

—Tony Orlando, musician
People's Choice Awards winner, three-time American
Music Award winner, Seven Seals Award winner,
"Tie a Yellow Ribbon Round the Ole Oak Tree" #1
in Billboard Hot 100 for four weeks in a row

Through the tears of hardship, pain, and sorrow come the overpowering rays of hope, healing, and wholeness from the steadfast life of my dear friend Cindi Lombardo. I am honored to recommend the reading of this book to all who honestly desire the character of God.

—Bruce Haynes, pastor
New Life Temple, Hollister, MO
Grammy nominated, Dove Award winner, seven-time
Male Vocalist, four-time Songwriter of the Year, "Praise
His Name" Song of the Decade, nine #1 songs, "I Need You
More" Top 100 Worship Songs, Living Legend Award

I am extremely honored to recommend the incredible book, *That's My God.* I have had the privilege of knowing members of Cindi's family for many years. They are people who are dedicated to serving God and people. Cindi is a remarkable lady who has given her life to reaching the world for Christ. I wish every human being on planet Earth had a copy of *That's My God* in his or her hands. This book is destined to change lives. It is powerful, it is beautifully written, it is anointed of the Holy Spirit, and it testifies of the majesty of our God. Open your heart and spirit as you open this book, and get ready to go on a spiritual journey that will change your life. You will not be the same person when you finish *That's My God*. God bless you.

Warning: This book will have an eternal effect upon your life.
—*Dr. Walt Spradling, senior pastor,*
CrystalRock Cathedral, Ardmore, OK

That's My God will bless every reader with every page they turn. Pastor Cindi's life continues to inspire and remind me "to love, even when it doesn't make sense and to believe and experience God's love as stronger than any setback life hurls at you." This book will cause your heart to marvel at Jesus while it provokes faith in your heart to see His power in your own life and the lives of those you hold dear.
—*Diane Bickle, founder & CEO of Glad Heart Realty,*
Co-founder, International House of Prayer, Kansas City, MO

I have known Cindi Lombardo for several years and have walked with her through some of her most difficult days. Cindi has an awesome, bubbly personality and has always lived her life large—large joys and incredibly large pain!

When I started reading the advance copy, I experienced a "couldn't put it down" feeling! This beautiful young woman loved her God, loved her husband, and loved her two sons with the deepest kind of love. Her life was a wonderful storybook spiritual journey. Then, suddenly in a moment, a knock at the door, and her husband and two sons were gone through a tragic accident. You will never be the same as you read her story! It will impact and change your life! You will learn, through Cindi's deep relationship with her God, how to triumph after tragedy! She has traveled around the world filling invitations to share her story. Our world desperately needs the incredible truths skillfully presented in *That's My God.*

—Dennis Slavens, founding pastor
Antioch Church, Overland Park, KS

With a purity that speaks to the heart of the doubting, faithless, or faith weary, *That's My God* is a written testimony of lives lived well here on earth. Lives that were intentional every day, to love everyone and anyone with sincerity, grace, and compassion.

This book is just what we all need to jump-start our dying hearts and breathe love, joy, and faith into our everyday realities. The reader who comes across this book will be forever changed, challenged, inspired, and set free on a journey that they never anticipated…FAITH!

—Dara Ann DeSoto, missionary to El Salvador*

Being a good friend of Nino and Giuseppe's, I was there before and after April 16. This is a real, raw, and heartfelt account of life that Pastor Cindi is pouring out in the pages of this book. The life she leads is beyond extraordinary and is what a "life of adventure lived in Christ" looks like. She is one of the most authentic and strong women I have ever met, and you will be blessed by reading this book.

This book is an electric and honest account of the sorrow and joy life brings, and how God can carry you through the hardest times of your life. This book is the epitome of courage, and because this life-trial is experienced and shared, it transcends pain and loss and becomes an inspiration. Pastor

Cindi is one of the bravest, most likeable, and sincerest loving women I have ever met. Her stories and lessons have such depth and will challenge and inspire you…if you are listening.

—Bo Nelson,* co-founder, Thou Mayest Coffee Roasters,
Recipient of Nino and Giuseppe Lombardo
Scholarship (2004), member of the Knights

Having known Pastor Cindi throughout her marriage to Butch, and being close friends with Nino and Guiseppe, I got a firsthand account of the love in their home and the testimony for God in the way they lived their everyday lives. Pastor Cindi has truly lived a life full of miracles and the power of God, exuding love and joy everywhere she goes, making her magnetic to all she encounters.

As you read through these pages, you'll realize the life she lives is truly an authentic testimony and proclamation of God's wonders and love. *That's My God* is full of the heart-wrenching account of the beautiful love and tremendous heartbreak Pastor Cindi has endured in this life, all while faithfully being watched over by God. She transparently uses her experience to show the depth and wonder of God's love for His children. As you read this book full of the stories of her life, there is no doubt you will be amazed and inspired by the journey she has walked and the strength she exudes!

—Shana Nicole Nelson,* friend of Guiseppe and Nino
Member of My Sister's House

If you are reading this and you do not know this family, you will be tempted to think these stories are embellished. I went to high school with Guiseppe and Nino and was one of the founding members of the Knights. I assure you these stories are real, and God is real. This book will touch many, many, many lives from non-believers to Christians alike, parents and children, male and female. God will reveal something to you when you read this book. And then you, too, will be saying, "That's My God."

—*Brien Reinke,* * *firefighter engineer/EMT*
Guiseppe's friend and fellow Knight

No matter where you find yourself in your journey with the Lord, you will be inspired by *That's My God*. Pastor Cindi lives a life of unique and captivating faith. As a woman who has experienced unimaginable heartache, she has a true God-given gift to lift the spirits of the masses. By the end of the book, your faith will have been deepened and your heart will be exclaiming alongside Pastor Cindi, *That's My God!*

—*Amy Christine Holzhueter,* * *friend of Guiseppe and Nino*
Member of My Sister's House

That's My God inspired us to appreciate what we have and gave us the motivation to trust God in moments when He dances beyond the bounds of our logic. We can't wait for our twins to read *That's My God*.

—*Anthony & Waheeda* * *Muti, one of the young*
ladies that grew up around the house

That's My God is more than a book full of stories about a woman and her family; it is a treasure chest full of simple life principles to raise a godly family who bring the pure gospel and love of Jesus to the world around them.

—*Anna Mason,* * *friend of Guiseppe and Nino*
Member of My Sister's House

I read *That's My God* in one sitting. The relationship Cindi has with God is amazing. The way He sustains her and is with her in every way she lives is an incredible gift that I desire to have in my own life.

Every mother needs to read this book. They all need Cindi's strength. God is with Cindi, and I am looking forward to reading *That's My God* again and again.

—*Francis Saluto, family*

That's My God shimmers with truth and dazzles with hope. It brings to life the compelling story of a woman amidst tremendous tragedy who chose joy over sorrow. This story calls us to open our hearts to love the life we live…the good, the bad, and even the sad. It invites us to love others, to start raising up future generations, and to believe that anything is possible with God.

—*Colleen Kirk,* * *student of My Father's Barn*
Member of My Sister's House

The boys (Guiseppe & Nino) were larger than life because that is the definition of eternity. These stories of their lives, and Butch and Cindi's, serve one purpose in my mind: to continue to point to the saving power of Christ.

—*Peter Freund,* * *close friend to Guiseppe and Nino,*
Member of the Knights

This book will challenge you. It will challenge you to believe and trust with childlike faith in a limitless Father. It will challenge you to not only endure in the face of suffering, but also to overcome. It will challenge you to learn to hear the voice of the Shepherd and obey when He speaks. It will challenge you to live every day for the glory of God.

I had the amazing privilege of knowing Nino, Guiseppe, and Butch. I remember when a friend invited me to the Lombardo's house for the first time. My friend was describing the Lombardo family to me. He told me they were the most loving people he had ever met and assured me they would treat me like family the moment I walked through their door. As he raved about them, I remember thinking they could not be as perfect as he made them sound and then fearing I would somehow be the one person they would not like. Those thoughts were quickly quelled when I was greeted with a big embrace from Nino at the door and was suddenly being introduced by Guiseppe to everyone as his friend. This family has been a treasure to me ever since that day, and I cannot say enough about how they have impacted my life. I can trace so many significant moments in my relationship with my heavenly Father back to Cindi and her men. I pray you would welcome the stories told in this book into your heart the way they welcomed me into their home. If you do, I believe you, too, will be forever changed.

—*Andrew Zarda, attorney*
Recipient of the Nino and Guiseppe
Lombardo Scholarship 2005

*Some of the girls and guys who were like family and grew up around the Lombardo household.

A TRUE LIFE STORY

THAT'S MY GOD

CINDI LOMBARDO

THAT'S MY GOD

I dedicate this book to my three men, Butch, Guiseppe, and Nino, who left a legacy of love.

Contents

Foreword

From the very moment I met Cindi, my life was forever changed. Traditionally, when you first meet someone you shake hands and acknowledge the person's presence. Our first meeting was more like getting swept up in a tornado of stories, passion, excitement, and a tangible, effervescent, nurturing love. The spirit was so strong and her guidance so on point that being around her forever changed the way I perceived myself and what was possible in a life.

Shortly after meeting, we found ourselves in Zimbabwe, Africa, where I witnessed my first miracles and felt the Spirit move in a profound, pervasive, and exacting manner. Our trip to Africa was the beginning of many adventures and life-changing moments I am forever grateful for. When you are with Cindi, things happen!

Cindi is an anomaly. Being a professional musician and entertainer, I have met and performed for millions of people all over the world—rich, poor, famous, and unknown. But never in my life have I met anybody like Cindi. To be stretched to the very depths of your emotional capacity and to still be unquestionably all-in for God is a profound statement of her complete love and faith in God.

Her walk and life are beyond words, but if you had to nail it down to one phrase it would be *salvation by surrender*. She is a shining example of what happens when you let go of everything and become nothing but a pure, open vessel. No judgment—just pure love and an undying willingness to serve our heavenly Father. She is one of a kind and forever my friend, counselor, and hero.

She is the reason I am the man I am today, and the reason I was able to complete the vision God gave me when I was eight years old of my wife-to-be. Not a day goes by that I do not thank God for her in my life. Read her story, and you will be forever changed as well.

Dominic Haygood, international recording artist
and father of four - soon to be six!

CHAPTER 1

Mom, you need to hear this!

Friday, April 16, 2004, started so special, as I remembered twenty-six years earlier when I held my firstborn son, Guiseppe, in my arms for the first time.

Birthday celebrations at our house always began with a birthday breakfast. In the evening, I would cook the birthday boy's dinner of choice. After dinner, the guys could have friends over if they wanted.

That morning I stood at the kitchen stove, and as the sun was waking up, so were my three men. I was preparing the birthday breakfast: eggs, bacon, and hash browns. I knew my men would be downstairs soon, and I could hardly contain my excitement. I began singing "Happy Birthday to You" as I added the final touches to the hash browns.

Our family looked at birthdays in a special way. Our celebration never centered on being with friends or getting presents. Instead, it was about giving thanks to God as a family for the life He had given. As parents, this was our time to speak into our sons' lives about the things of God and the callings He had placed on their lives. We always reminded them there was really only one reason they were here on earth and that was to point the way to Jesus Christ. They were on this earth to show the love of God to all they would see and meet.

As breakfast cooked, I began to put the guys' lunch coolers together. I pulled the homemade bread out of the oven to let it cool for their sandwiches. Then I cut up some carrots. They loved everything fresh.

It was never a burden for me to prepare meals for my family. I loved it! I knew who I was in Christ. My joy was complete, and I was fulfilled in being His child. I didn't battle with the lying minefield the world throws at young women—Who am I? What is my role in life? I knew I was a child of the King, and I knew my call was to love and support my family unit.

Every woman who walks in her calling is fulfilled, and it is joyful to her. It is not work. I was in my calling. I had been given the power and authority by the Holy Ghost to bring love, peace, and joy into our home, and it was my pleasure in life to serve my men as I would serve Christ.

I finished getting things on the table. The plates, silverware, napkins, and water glasses were set. Vitamins were placed next to each plate, and four Bibles were set to the side. A bouquet of flowers my sons had given me on the previous Friday sat in the center of the table. The coffee was brewed. Everything was ready.

I took a moment to thank the Lord for blessing me with such a wonderful family. I thought, If everything were gone tomorrow, I know I have lived a life of no regrets. The thought surprised me and I paused for a moment. "Lord, I have a fullness in You, and I understand my call and the love You have for me. I have tried to live a life of no regrets."

Just then, Guiseppe came down the stairs. He gave me a hug and a kiss. "Thanks, Mom!" he said, as he smelled what was cooking. He was always so grateful and so full of love. He never took anything I did for granted.

Guiseppe saw his gifts and said, "Which one is from you, Momma? Can I shake it?" He picked up a gift and shook it.

"Get your hands off that!" I said, laughing.

Joy filled Guiseppe that morning. He started singing and pulled me over to dance with him. "Momma, you're my best girl!" He smiled, then picked me up and twirled me around one more time. "Anything I can help you with, Momma?"

At that moment, Nino, my other son, came charging down the stairs.

"Happy birthday, brother." He gave Guiseppe a hug and a kiss on both sides of his face. The kiss was always on both sides of the face. When they were little, they saw verses in the Bible that said, "Greet one another with a holy kiss" (see Romans 16:16, 2 Corinthians 13:12, and 1 Thessalonians 5:26). They saw Jewish men kiss this way and said, "That's it."

Nino headed into the kitchen. He could probably smell the bread I had baked. Nino loved food!

"Where's my girl?" Nino burst out. "You know I love you, Momma," he said, as he gave me a kiss. He spotted the bread and immediately started pulling off pieces to taste.

A moment later, my husband, Butch, entered the kitchen. "Good morning, baby." He gave me a kiss. "How's the love of my life this morning?"

The house always had an atmosphere of love and joy.

I got the biscuits from the oven as the guys grabbed their seats. I joined them at the table and we all took hands to pray. Butch said the blessing.

"Dear Lord, I ask that You would bless my sons today, and help them to make the right decisions, and protect their eyes from any evil thing. I ask You to raise them up as righteous and holy men. Let them always see those who are in need. May they be Your arms and Your smile and give Your love to those who feel no love. May they have words to lift up the brokenhearted. Guard them, Lord Jesus, from straying from Your path. Amen."

As we finished the meal, we opened our Bibles. We all knew the Scripture for the day would be Proverbs 16 because it was Guiseppe's birthday. Butch and I taught the boys that they each had their own chapter of Proverbs. The number of chapters in the book of Proverbs matches the number of days in a month, and we encouraged the boys to memorize and study the chapter that lined up with the day they were born.

Butch began reading. "The preparations of the heart belong to man, but the answer of the tongue is from the LORD." We all listened as Butch read the chapter.

"So what did you get out of that?" Butch asked the boys when he finished reading.

Guiseppe and Nino shared their thoughts and discussed what verses they felt God highlighting in their hearts that day. My heart swelled with pride for my boys, now men, and the way they honored both their earthly and heavenly Fathers.

As I cleared the table, the guys gathered their things and grabbed their lunches. With the love of God filling their hearts, they each gave me a kiss as they headed out the door. That morning, like many before, was a beautiful reflection of the holy Father's love for my family and me.

My sons and husband climbed into the car and said a quick prayer before pulling out of the driveway. "Lord give us eyes like an eagle to look with a sharp eye for those who need You this day, that we may be used by You. Amen!"

I went to the sink and washed the dishes, then began getting the house ready for the day. A few moments later, Nino rushed back into the house. I thought he must have forgotten something.

"Momma?" he said as he pushed open the door.

"Yes," I answered. "I thought you guys left."

"We did. I had Dad stop and turn the car around to come back to the house. I had to tell you something and felt I needed to say it face to face." Nino looked very serious. "Momma, I had to come back and tell you that you're the most submissive woman I know."

"Well, thank you, Nino." I looked at him, thinking how cute it was that he had come back just to tell me that.

"Momma, it takes a lot of strength to die to yourself and love serving the three of us."

Again I said, "Thank you, Nino!"

He went on. "Momma, people don't know how strong you are. They don't know how you hear God and how you know the Word." He looked at me with a fire in his eyes, and I realized this was more than just a cute moment.

"Thank you, Nino," I responded again, but this time with more seriousness in my voice. Nino was always passionate, but this particular morning I could see there was something weighing on him.

"You're the best mom in the world. You really need to hear me say I love you!"

I was thinking how sweet this was of him. He could see this on my face, and he grabbed me by the shoulders, looked me in the eyes, and said, "Listen, Momma, you need to hear this like it's the last time you will hear it."

I smiled, so proud of his heart wanting to let me know his sincerity. "Alright," I answered.

Nino embraced me and said again, "I love you." Then he turned and headed back out the door.

I went about my day as usual.

At 3:30 that afternoon, I answered a knock at the front

door. The words I heard changed my world in one blinding moment.

"There are no survivors, ma'am...."

Chapter 2

I Am Loved

As a child, I saw everything as sunshine, lollipops, and rainbows. It didn't matter what was going on around me, I always saw the sunshine coming through. I was born into a wonderful family with three beautiful sisters, each one of us unique in our own way.

Sharon Elaine was the firstborn. We called her Cher because of the popularity of Sonny and Cher at the time. I remember Sharon having all the answers. She was Daddy's dainty little blue-eyed girl. Yep. She was Daddy's little girl! How many dads come home to find their eleven-year-old daughter has cut a hole in the garage ceiling and created a pulley system to hoist an engine out of a car? That was my sister Cher. Whenever Dad had the hood of a car open, she was right there, sitting on the bumper, just waiting to get her hands dirty. Sharon has always been mechanically inclined. She's so smart and loves knowing how things work. She *is* the complete book of *Common Sense*, Volumes 1–4.

TK is next. She is so insightful and has such an ability to read people. To me, it seemed like TK always had a plan. I remember how she noticed that my grandpa could never say no when Connie, our youngest sister, asked him for something. One day, TK convinced Connie to ask Grandpa to to take us to get ice cream. While Connie went to ask, we waited on the old porch swing of my grandparents' wonderful two-story farmhouse on the hill. The next thing we knew, Grandpa was driving down the long driveway with Connie in his truck to go get ice cream. Our mouths dropped as we realized something was missing in the message. Connie was only four, and I am sure she said something like "Grandpa, can I have some ice cream?" When Grandpa and Connie got back, she rushed over to us, ice cream in hand. "TK, you were right. It worked!"

"Not exactly," explained TK. "You were supposed to ask him to take all of us!"

TK has such a presence about her. She can walk into a room and change the atmosphere. She is so compassionate and has helped an endless number of people. You cannot be around her and not be inspired. I have always called her a peacock, not just because of her fiery red hair, but because a peacock never enters a room unnoticed. Everyone notices when TK enters the room because she exudes a commanding personality.

Connie is the youngest. How can I describe this sister of mine without crying? I don't think it's possible! We have been so close all our lives. She was my closest friend growing up. She was the one everyone *oohed* and *aahed* about. When she came into a room, she delighted absolutely everyone with her dimples, blonde hair, big brown eyes, and great sense of humor. Connie always knew how to get me laughing.

One day at church, when I was about ten years old, Connie gave me the play-by-play of Sister Stevens' eye cleaning. Sister Stevens—at our church we called everyone *sister* or *brother*—had a glass eye, and during every service, without fail, she would plop it out to clean it.

"It's out," Connie whispered. "She's got it in her hankie."

I started to giggle.

"She just put it in her mouth! She's shining it up and rolling it around....Left cheek...Now right."

I could barely keep myself from bursting out laughing.

"Oops. She spit it back into the hankie. And...She put it back in. All clean."

By now Connie and I were giggling out loud. Sister Stevens must have heard us because she turned around right then to give us a scolding look.

"Oh! She put it in backwards!" Connie said.

Yep. Sister Stevens had put her glass eye in backwards.

I lost it. Connie and I laughed so hard. Not a silent giggle, but a belly laugh. This behavior was not the kind that blessed our very quiet mother who did not want attention drawn her way. Mother quietly snapped her finger, then shook it while giving us *the look*—eyebrow downward, lips pursed together, head shaking as if to say, "What am I going to do with those two?"

Along with my three sisters, I also had an older brother named Timmy. He was actually my uncle, my mom's brother. However, he was far more like a brother than an uncle to my sisters and me. When my momma was eleven years old, her mother died. At the time, Timmy was only three. My mother always wanted him with her. So from the time I can remember, he lived with us. My parents cared for him, and my sisters and I always thought of him as our older brother.

Dad would take us on road trips to see his family in Shiloh, Illinois. As we went down the highway, he and Momma would sing "The Old Rugged Cross," "In the Garden," or "Mansion Over the Hilltop." Oh, how I loved those car trips. What special times we had.

We were seven people living in a one-bedroom house without electricity. Sometimes my parents were a little late paying the utilities, or rent, or the kitchen cabinets were a little low on food, but we were never low on love. We children may have gotten our backsides spanked from time to time, but we knew without a doubt we were loved. I remember our home as a place of joy and peace.

God's Little Sunshine

My mother called me her little sunshine. I thought if she saw me that way, my heavenly Father probably felt the same.

When I was four, I remember wearing TK's dress. It had a brown and white checkered pattern on it and a white Peter Pan collar. I thought it was the most beautiful dress in the whole world. It was definitely the best we had. I went outside, leaned against the garage door, and looked toward the sky. With my four-year-old heart, I know, without a doubt, I saw the Father looking at me. His eyes were smiling at me, and I could hear clear as a bell "You look pretty in that dress. I love you, Cindi." Love flowed through me.

To this day, I can still see it all clearly. I curtsied for Him by pulling my dress out like I would bow before a king. In that moment, I felt sparkles come down all around me, landing on my face, feeling cold and wet at the same time. They tickled me and made me laugh. I knew my heavenly Father was smiling down on me. I knew He loved my dress. I knew He loved how I felt about the dress.

I remember being completely overwhelmed by His love for me. I could feel the intensity of His love flowing from His eyes. That love washed all over me as a little girl, and the very thought of how much He loved me brought me to tears. It was so real I still get tears in my eyes when I think about it to this day. It shakes me in my heart and reminds me to reverence my heavenly Father, who delights in His little girl. I know what I felt came down from heaven above and landed all over me that day. It was the pure delight of my heavenly Father. And I still know my heavenly Father delights over me!

Once, in my fourth-grade year at school, Satan tried to attack my self-worth by attacking my looks. I had a tiny breakout of blemishes on my face, and a classmate laughed at me and called me "Pizza Face." A few days later, my looks were attacked again. My teacher had become upset with me, and I started to cry. She told me to stop crying and said I had the ugliest face she had ever seen. She held me up in front of the whole class, and then turned me to a cabinet with a mirror so I could see my face.

"Look! Look at the ugliest face in the world," she said.

Her words pierced my heart. I looked at my face and learned it was the ugliest face in the world. I was in shock as I looked in the mirror.

That night in bed I asked God to give me a face people could love. I asked that when I smiled, people would see Jesus and not me, and that through my smile they would literally feel the love He has for them. Right then, as a fourth-grade child, I felt His presence in my room. God's glory filled that room and comforted a little girl and made her feel safe in her pain. I felt like a special treasure to the Lord.

God answered my prayer. Oh yes. Do you know how I knew? When I went to church the next Sunday, people came up to me and told me they could see Jesus in my smile! It didn't matter what was on the outside. I don't know how big I must have been smiling. I used to smile all the time and no one commented before, but after I prayed, I started hearing it all the time from people who spoke to me. What happened that night became a milestone in my life.

Many times after that encounter I felt God's presence fill my room again. God would come and love on me, and He would bring me back to that moment with Him when I was four. I would ask Him that people would be able to feel His love around me. I would ask that those who were hurting would feel His love, and it would heal their brokenness. From that time on, I believe there was a real spirit of love around me. I hated seeing people hurt or in pain, and I think I had a sense, even at that young age, of how God wanted to love people through my life.

I believe the Lord Himself coached me through negative ways of thinking and gave me revelation on how much He loved and protected me.

During a stage in my schooling, my grades were terrible, and I was called stupid. I had a speech impediment and couldn't say words with *r* in them. Teachers wanted to keep me back. Instead, I left my class for an hour for speech impediment classes every day for two years. Many times the enemy has tried to use an event or struggle to define me in my thinking and has tried to steal who I really was. Satan tries to take us out early in life. He wants to steal, kill, and destroy (see John 10:10). But God has the final say and tells us who we really are!

I hope you know God is speaking to you. He has so much to say about how He loves you! Maybe He has been speaking to you, and you just need this little reminder to listen and believe His ways and His love. People can try to discount someone's experiences with God, but God has revealed Himself to me in so many tangible ways I could never doubt His love and faithfulness toward me.

CHAPTER 3

How I Learned to Overcome

As the Vietnam war raged, my brother Timmy enlisted into the Navy. I was in the second grade at the time. In 1968, we received a telegram saying he would soon be home from Vietnam. We were all excited to see him again.

Timmy was serving on the aircraft carrier *USS Kearsarge*. The same day we received the telegram, the carrier docked in California, and the crew began their final sweep of the ship. A superior officer ordered Timmy to roll up a large air hose. Meanwhile, another crew member went to cut off the air pressure. When the man went to shut the hose off, he accidentally turned the valve the wrong way. The hose went up to 5,000 pounds of pressure almost instantly. Timmy was in the middle of rolling up the hose, and the increased air pressure launched both the hose and Timmy into the air. In a moment of quick thinking, he attempted to let go of the hose and dive off the side of the ship. He made it over the edge of the ship, but what he had not seen was the barge that had pulled alongside of the ship. He landed head first onto the barge. The fall broke his neck and shattered his spine.

Timmy returned home in a wheelchair, a quadriplegic. The fall paralyzed him from the neck down, and he had absolutely no feeling in his body. He looked so different when we saw him, but Momma and Daddy told us we needed to be strong for him. Because it would be so much work to care for Timmy, the Navy encouraged my parents to leave him in the veteran's hospital. The thought of leaving him there was not an option in their minds. From that day on, my parents cared for Timmy. They fed him, bathed him, and dressed him. Every day they would try to figure out new ways to help make Timmy's day better for him.

The accident completely impacted my outlook on life. My parents were living to serve. My sisters and I quickly learned from their example. We helped around the house and took time to love on Timmy. We learned there was a place on his cheek about the size of a quarter where he still had feeling. We would put our hands on his cheek and kiss his face. Through this experience, we learned to recognize the needs of those around us and not to focus on ourselves.

Self-pity and complaining were not allowed at my house. Anytime we felt like things were tough for us, all we had to do was look at our parents and Timmy. They showed us what it means to endure until the end. They never had an attitude of giving up or throwing in the towel.

There was no saying *can't* in our home. If you even thought of going to Momma and saying, "Momma, I can't do this," she would say, "Timmy can't walk. Now, can you do this?"

"Yes, Momma, I can." And that was the end of that subject.

My parents showed me how to endure, but they also taught me how to have hope and to trust God to do great things. I was raised in a church where the move of God was expected, rather than unusual. When I was a child, I was exposed to a wooden barrel full of prosthetics. My favorite was a wooden prosthetic foot with a name and date on it. The name was the name of the man who had received a real foot from God and no longer needed the prosthesis; the date was the day he received it. One Sunday, I saw a man my whole family knew personally, whose eyes had been blown out while fighting overseas, receive new eyes. **That's my God!**

I am so thankful my momma and daddy took us to this church as often as they did so we could be exposed to the supernatural power of God. It was a Bible-believing church that spoke the Word, saved souls, and healed people. They sent people out to preach the gospel and helped plant Bible colleges all over the world. The church never wanted any big news flash about themselves—the name of Jesus was the only name they wanted receiving the glory.

Believing for Myself

When I was fifteen years old, I struggled severely with my menstrual cycles. I fainted regularly and also passed blood clots of such significant weight that it concerned the doctors greatly. I started bleeding more and more days each month—I would bleed two weeks in a month and then as much as three weeks a month, like a woman who was in her change of life. It was an extremely difficult time.

One day as I was cheerleading at a football game, I collapsed and was rushed to the hospital. The doctor said all my female organs would have to be removed. He said I had the ovaries of an eighty-year-old. That they needed to be removed immediately or it would be extremely dangerous for my body. Obviously, this meant I would never be able to have children of my own. I was devastated. I didn't understand. I had seen God heal so many people. Our family had always trusted God for healing, so why would He not do it for me? The hospital staff prepared me for surgery and started wheeling me down the hall.

"Momma," I cried out. "You believe God can heal! What about me?"

Later, when I woke up, the doctors were sitting there with Momma and me. They looked at me and said, "Your mother stopped us from going through with the surgery. She stopped us from doing what was best for you."

Oh, no she didn't! Momma did what God said was best and stopped the surgery. She believed God could heal me, and I left the hospital believing He had. An outsider might have thought nothing had changed. I continued to have long monthly cycles, during which I would pass blood clots and often pass out. But I knew something was different. I believed God had healed me.

Four years later, I sat in a doctor's office listening to the doctor say, "I don't know how this happened. I don't want to get your hopes up, but all the tests indicate that you are pregnant." The doctors had said it was medically impossible. But **that's my God!** All things are possible with Him! After I gave birth to Guiseppe, everything changed. No more long cycles, no more passing out, no more large blood clots every month. It was over. Yes, thank You, Jesus!

When I was twenty-one years old and going to Bible college, another student who grew up next door to us told me we were one of the poorest families they knew. As far as I was concerned our home was perfect, and we had everything we needed. I loved that we all lived and slept so close together. I never thought of us as being poor.

My mom was in that Bible class with me, and on break, getting coffee I asked, "Really, Momma, were we poor?"

"No, honey," Momma said. "We were not poor. They are just talking about money."

We may not have had much money, but my parents made

sure we never felt poor. They made sure we knew we were loved, and that covers pretty much every need.

I love the very thought of my childhood. Did my family go through rough times? You bet, and that is what gave us the strength to be who we are. As I sit here writing, I am singing the lyrics of a great old Lanny Wolfe song that tells us to praise God's name in the good times, bad times, and in everything give Him thanks.

Without rough times, you have no need to search out the Father's mercy and grace and deepen your relationship with Him. I am not saying that God puts us in bad times. No, the devil is bad, and God is good. All the time! I just mean that rough seasons are an opportunity to offer up a sacrifice of praise and seek the Lord even more fervently. Trials give us an opportunity to witness God's character and faithfulness in ways we might not otherwise.

My Father in heaven was certainly smiling over me throughout my childhood. He still is. He gets a big kick out of me! I make Him laugh so sweetly sometimes that it makes me laugh. I know I am more than a conqueror, and I can do all things through Jesus Christ who gives me strength!

CHAPTER 4

When I Fell in Love

In March 1973, I was sitting in my dining room doing homework at the table when, suddenly, I saw my handsome prince walk through the door. At that moment, it was as though the whole earth stood still. As he looked at me with those big brown eyes I knew he was mine! I could hardly catch my breath. My face flushed. My eyes teared up and my heart raced. I couldn't look at him. I immediately put my eyes to the floor because I didn't want him to see my face turn red.

He had a very quiet spirit, and I could tell right from the beginning he understood honor. He had the presence of greatness on him—something kingly and strong, yet dignified. He entered the room with quiet confidence, sure of himself.

Now can you see why I had eyes only for him? He quite simply took my breath away! With that one look, he quietly grabbed hold of my heart from across the room, and I knew that place in my heart was sold! I declared my heart *Off the Market*. I knew there was room for no one else.

Kevin McKibben, a friend from high school, had dropped by our house to use our phone book and brought a friend in with him. Kevin had moved to our town earlier that year. His friend had driven fifty miles to come visit him. Shortly after using the phone book, they left.

Though a brief encounter, neither Butch nor I ever forgot that day. He would later tell our sons how he remembered exactly what I was wearing—a black sweater and black and white checkered pants. It was quite funny to hear the two of us tell the story together. Butch would say, "I thought she was beautiful, but I had no thoughts about marriage." I, on the other hand, could already see us walking down the aisle. Yes, girls, it's true. I was fifteen years old, and from the moment I saw him, bells were ringing and plans were forming, and I am almost certain birds were flying over my head like in a Disney movie. "I think my bridesmaids should wear pink," I would say to myself. "Hmm, wait a minute. I don't even know his name!"

Eventually, I learned his given name: Joseph D. M. Lombardo Jr. He was sixteen years old and his nickname was Butch. The next time I saw Butch was months later, in the summer. Kevin was dating my sister TK at the time, and Butch was visiting again. He and Kevin were horseback riding, and they rode up to my sisters and me to say hi. They chatted with us for a little while and then rode off again. Butch exuded such inner peace and strength, and I'd never known anyone like that before. All right, call me a hopeless romantic, but in my fifteen years nobody had ever had this effect on me before. I was even surprised at my own reaction. My heart was pounding as I watched him ride off into the distance, certain I could hear theme music from some western movie. I didn't know when I would see him again.

On February 22, 1974, I turned sixteen. My sisters and I were all cheerleaders, and it was a big Friday night basketball game. At halftime, my sisters asked me to stay up in the bleachers with the crowd and just watch a routine they had

prepared. I was disappointed they had organized an entire routine without including me, but they said they had a surprise
for me. So I agreed to watch from the stands. The cheerleaders
passed out wax paper and combs to parents in the crowd so
they could hum through them with the beat of the song.

As my sisters and the rest of the squad ran down to the
main floor, I heard the announcer say, "Tonight we have a
surprise! Cindi Manning is turning sixteen, and the cheerleading squad has prepared a dance routine just for her."

All of the cheerleaders began dancing to the hit song
"You're Sixteen (You're Beautiful and You're Mine)." Apparently, while this performance was taking place, my husband-
to-be was walking into Lansing High School to watch Kevin
play the second half of his varsity basketball game. That
night was when Butch really noticed me. How could he not?
The whole school was singing to me. Now, isn't that a great
girl moment? I didn't see Butch, but he certainly saw me. I
could never have arranged that to work out so perfectly, but
that's my God!

I was sixteen for a whole month before I saw Butch again.
My daddy allowed his daughters to start dating at sixteen,
and we had a school dance coming up. Kevin and TK were
going together, and Kevin wanted me to go with Butch since
Butch was coming to visit. TK called me at the drugstore
where I worked and asked if I wanted to go to the dance
with a friend of Kevin's named Butch.

"Do you remember him, Cindi?" she asked.

What a question! Of course I remembered him. My heart
started pounding all over again.

Daddy said I could go if all the sisters went, and Butch
would have to dance with each one of us. So Butch did just
that. At the dance, when I was busy dancing with him for

the third time, I said, "I don't know if you know this or not, but I'm your date." He replied my sisters had informed him, so yes, he knew I was his date. I was so relieved. Whew!

I had a wonderful time, but I got weak in the knees or glassy-eyed whenever I looked at him for too long. I felt embarrassed because I struggled to get control of my emotions. I could not look straight at him. I was definitely not ready for all this emotion—just looking at him affected my whole being.

Butch and I continued seeing each other after the dance. Now, as a young girl, I certainly could have let my emotions get carried away. But I am thankful to say my sisters, my dad, my mom, and Timmy helped me keep it real. After all, you can't be anything but real when you date with your family around. I often requested we take Timmy or Connie along with us on our dates. And Butch loved doing things with my family. We often sat around with my family and played games and visited together. Getting to know Butch this way helped me to be myself and stay covered with wisdom from my parents. Plus, if I tried any goofy girl stuff, someone in the family would detect it and nail me for putting up a front.

I knew from the start Butch was my future husband. He had a very quiet and yet confident presence. When he entered a room, he took it over—not by force but by a peace and surety of who he was. He had a gentle and yet strong, kingly spirit about him. With one look, he could reach hold of my heart from across the room. I was totally his.

143 (I Love You)

Our courtship days were beautiful—we were crazy about each other. For the first five months we were not even allowed to hold hands, but when we were finally given permission,

I felt like a firecracker about to go off. One night we were sitting at the dinner table with my family, and I kept taking his hand over and over. My parents told me I was being too passionate and put me back on restriction from holding hands with Butch.

"Dear, we just got permission to hold hands, and now we're already on restriction. Just calm down," Butch said.

I was sixteen years old, and had never felt this way before. I think my parents could see how hard I had fallen for this guy. I constantly told Butch I loved him. There was never any doubt in my mind about that.

Butch wrote the most extraordinary love letters to me all the time. About a year into our relationship, he began to suspect I was reading these amazing letters out loud to my sisters. And I was. I admired him so much, and I wanted my family to see what an amazing man he was. Butch wanted the letters to be private, so when he found out, he asked that I stop reading them aloud. I agreed. From that point on, I read the letters to myself. When I finished reading, I passed the letters on so my sisters could read them silently, too.

One weekend, he came to the house, and Connie mentioned something to him about one of his letters. He came to me and said, "Dear, I thought I asked you to stop reading my letters out loud to your sisters."

"I did."

"Well, Connie just spoke to me about something I wrote in the letter this week to you."

"I know, but I didn't read it to her; she read it herself. You see, no more reading it out loud. Now I just read a page and pass it. No more problem."

"Esther," he said to my mother, "did you hear this?"

"Oh, Cindi," Mom said. "He meant keep it to yourself."

I had no secrets in my life, so I thought Butch wanted my family to form their own opinions without my over-the-top-in-love inflections.

The letters were often a topic of conversation among us girls. Daddy and Momma thought the letters were getting a bit too passionate because of the many times he wrote *I love you*, so Butch and I agreed to be more careful at how we expressed our love to each other. He started writing *1-4-3* on our love notes. I couldn't figure out what it meant. My first thought was that it must be some sort of mathematical code because Butch was so intelligent. I never thought to ask what it meant.

One day he came over to the house, and I got emotional. "Do you still love me?" I asked him.

"Yes, of course!"

"But you don't ever tell me anymore."

He looked at me and smiled. "I tell you all the time. I put it in all the letters. 1-4-3."

"What is that, your locker number?"

"No," he said. "One letter…four letters…three letters. I…love…you!"

He had been telling me he loved me the whole time. He wrote it on the outside of every envelope and on page after page after page. I didn't get it at first, but I certainly got it after that. 1-4-3 became our secret code. Every time after visiting, Butch would make a 1-4-3 with his fingers as he pulled out of the driveway.

After we dated about two years, Butch asked Daddy if he could marry me. Daddy already knew Butch was the man for me. Daddy told me the Lord had given him peace about my marrying Butch after we had been together for five months. So he had no hesitation in giving his blessing.

A few weeks later, Butch and I were walking on the Kansas City Plaza with my sisters, their dates, and one of my cousins. All of a sudden, Butch jumped up onto a wishing well. "Cindi Sue Manning, will you marry me?"

It was so unlike him to jump up like that in public, and I was sure he was feeling embarrassed for having done it, so I said, "Come down off of there, sweetie!"

"Well, aren't you going to answer me?" he persisted.

"It's a given!" I said. "Of course I'm going to marry you!"

We were married June 25, 1976, at the Tabernacle Church in Kansas City, one year after Butch proposed.

Man of Promise

While Butch and I were dating, he folded a $20 bill into a ring and slipped it on my finger.

"This twenty is in case of an emergency—for emergency use only." Butch did these kinds of things all the time to take care of me.

I was so excited! I wore the $20 bill ring to high school the next day and showed it off to all my friends in class. "Can you believe he said 'for emergency use only'?"

I got into trouble for being too showy. The teacher kicked me out of class and sent me to the principal's office because I refused to take it off. I told them it was only to be taken off "for emergency use" so they called my parents.

"Get that ring off your finger," Daddy and Momma said. "You're getting kicked out of school otherwise—this is your emergency!"

That day, Butch came over and found out I was going to get kicked out of school if I didn't take off the $20 ring. "That's all right," he said. "One day we'll have been married for twenty years, and I'll put that back on your finger in gold."

I thought he was so sweet for saying that.

Sure enough, on our twentieth anniversary, we were sitting with our two sons at a table at Macaroni Grill in Overland Park, Kansas. As Butch began to fold a crispy new $20 bill, he started telling the boys the story of the $20 ring. As he told the story, he continued to fold the $20 into a ring but it kept coming undone. He asked me to chime in and start telling parts of the story while he got another $20 bill. As I did, he slid a solid gold ring in the shape of the $20 one onto my finger.

"See, I told your mother that it would be twenty years and I would put that ring on her in gold."

He had a ring made for me, and on the inside he had inscribed *For emergency use only.* It was made from three wedding rings my grandfathers had passed onto me. Butch wanted me to have a ring that was unlike anyone else's in the whole world.

He was a man of promise, passion, and humility. He was a man of his word—when he said something, he meant it. And that was it!

CHAPTER 5

The Early Days of Marriage

Oh how I loved Butch, and I would learn to love him as Christ loved. I wanted Butch to know he could trust my love for him. I wanted him to have peace inside himself. So I prayed for these things, asking the Holy Spirit to help me love deeper and to love even when it did not make sense.

I realized men felt a heavy weight of responsibility in marriage, and Butch was mentally in a whole new groove in his mind. In the beginning, men are focused on the pursuit of a woman and winning her heart. Then their focus turns to providing. Butch had won my heart and now had to become the full-time provider for what he had won. He went from having responsibility for one, to being a nineteen-year-old man under the pressure of paying the rent, water, electricity, car payments, and insurance for two within one moment of saying "I do."

On top of this responsibility, he didn't want the fighting he had seen in other marriages. The only way he could think to avoid it was to be quiet. He sometimes went for weeks with limited conversation with me. It drove me crazy because I was so in love with him. Nothing he could have said could make me not love him. Once, I ran down the hall, jumped on him, and tried to pin him to the floor just to get him to talk to me.

"What are you doing?" he immediately yelled.

"Aha! I got you to talk to me!" That was my way of letting him know I was not going to let him pull into his own shell and hide from our marriage.

I was young, eighteen, and yet the Lord gave me wisdom and insight into my husband's fears. Butch was dealing with many of his own fears at that stage. He was afraid our marriage would end up in divorce like his parents' had.

I didn't desire our marriage to look like so many others that had lost their passion but remained married because they had signed a contract, so I fought for our love in prayer. The Lord showed me that marriage was an example of His love for us. If people can't see His love in us, if we're not loving each other, constantly uplifting one another, we begin to look like the world instead of a child of the King. Who are we going to draw to us if most of what they see in us is anger and bitterness?

I prayed that everything in me would show Butch the love of God. I so badly wanted him to believe how much I loved him was true that I would tell him over and over again. He was always suspicious when I said "I love you" because he thought I wanted something. As a child, he thought you only used the words "I love you" if you wanted something in return. I did not grow up receiving anything in return for those words except for love, so this was something I never understood. All I knew was I loved Butch and would not give up believing that the Lord was working in my husband's heart and using me to demonstrate His love.

I was so grateful to have grown up in a family where we never had an attitude of giving up. I watched my parents grow in the Spirit and never back down from a challenge. My brother, Timmy, who was in a wheelchair after a tragic accident returning home from the Vietnam war, made it hard to say, "I can't" when things got difficult. But my parents had always made it clear "I can't" was not in their vocabulary, and this instilled in me a strength and determination to never give up.

Butch didn't know what to do with my constant flood of love toward him. He began to feel like something was wrong with him, and eventually, the Holy Spirit revealed to him the fear and anger in his heart, and the need to forgive his father for divorcing his mother. After Butch forgave his father and submitted his fears to the Lord, it made our marriage even stronger. Butch often looked back at those early days and apologized for the way he treated me. I knew our marriage would never be like that again.

Seeing how much the Lord healed Butch's heart truly blessed me. The brokenness in him was now whole. He had become a warrior with a beautiful marriage that exemplified Christ.

Butch's Desire to Care for and Protect Me

Butch was a great man who always wanted to take care of me and never wanted me to worry. When we were first married, we lived in Dallas, Texas. One day, he was outside working on his car. He had been out there for a few hours. When he came in, I went to greet him, and a foul smell was coming off him.

"Is everything okay?" I asked.

He said yes and went on.

"Hey, sweetie, is everything alright?"

"Yes," he insisted.

"Did something catch on fire?"

"No!"

"Sweetie, I really hate to keep on asking, but are your sure there wasn't some kind of fire?"

He was sure! I asked him to come with me to the bathroom, turned on the light, and had him look in the mirror. We both started laughing. He said the battery had blown up in his face, and he didn't want me worried about it. It burnt off his eyebrows, his mustache, and his hair at the forehead area. His face was red like a bad sunburn. He stunk of burnt hair. It was so funny, and yet all I could do next was praise God he didn't lose his sight. Even his eyelashes were curled up from the heat.

It was quite something for him to marry someone like me who knew absolutely no privacy or secrecy! Everyone who knew the two of us said we were definitely a case of opposites attract, but I know it was God bringing a perfect team together. We learned so much from one another and complemented each other in the best possible ways.

Bible College

One day shortly after we were married, Butch and I were looking at our wedding photos. In the background of one picture on the wall of the church was a Scripture: "You shall know the truth, and the truth shall make you fr--." A vase of flowers hid the end of the verse and the Scripture reference. I had sat in that church my whole life and hadn't noticed that verse on the wall.

Butch saw that picture and couldn't stop asking me, "You shall know the truth, and the truth will make you *what? What, dear?*"

He picked up the large Bible given to us as a wedding gift and started reading every night, but he got more and more frustrated. He thought he had to start from the beginning of the book and read all the way through to find the verse. Months went by, and he got even more frustrated.

"I have to know where that verse is at," he told me.

"Call my Uncle Dick."

That's just what Butch did, and Uncle Dick immediately told Butch, "The truth shall set you free. It's John 8:32." They went into a deeper discussion, and Butch asked how he could learn more about the Bible. He wanted to know that no one was lying to him about God's Word. He was searching out how he was going to raise his sons. My Uncle Dick told him about Grace and Glory Bible College, a two-year college centered on studying the Word of God.

And so in 1977, Butch and I enrolled at Grace and Glory Bible College. Butch had to trade his high-paying job in Texas to move back to Kansas City and work all day at multiple jobs in order to go to this Bible college. After we graduated, the dean of the college came to Butch and said, "Butch, has the Lord been speaking to you about teaching at Grace and Glory?"

To my surprise, Butch responded yes. It was the first I had heard of it. Butch had heard the Lord calling him to teach for a couple of months but had not said anything. However, he believed if God was speaking to him about it, God would also speak to the dean. Butch often operated in this way. If God spoke to him about something that involved another person, Butch would wait until God spoke to that person, too. Butch never wanted to tell someone, "God is saying…" Instead, he wanted it to come from God as a confirmation.

At the age of twenty-three, Butch began teaching his first class on biblical prophecy: Ezekiel, Daniel, Revelation, all the Major and Minor Prophets. He was not content in blindly trusting any man's teaching, but studied the Bible for himself. He studied the Word three hours every night, and four hours on Sundays, praying and seeking God on how to teach. He would show all cross-references, studying all biblical resources, studies, and guides he could find. He would check with God on everything he studied and teach the revelation God gave in his heart. He saw everything in charts and graphs and would draw out what he studied into a graphical representation.

Butch taught at Grace and Glory for one year, taught his sons his whole life, and spoke at other churches throughout his life. He even went on to open Sower's Field Bible College, which still meets today at the barn behind the house.

Butch, the Man

Everyone who knew Butch, knew the two passions of his life, His Lord and Savior Jesus Christ and his family, which all who knew him became. I believe God instilled these passions in his heart at a very young age.

When Butch was just eight years old, God spoke to him. He was outside at recess playing basketball with two friends when all of a sudden, he audibly heard God's voice. Immediately he stopped playing, sat under a tree, and took in what the Lord told him. One of his friends came up to him and asked if he was okay.

"I just heard God speak to me," Butch said. He and his friend sat there under the tree and quietly honored the moment. Butch never told me exactly what God spoke to him that day, but he never forgot that moment and neither did his friends who were there. When Butch heard God speak, he knew God was real. He gave his heart to Jesus that very day.

Even from a young age, Butch was adamant about being truthful and honest. His brother said Butch couldn't lie even if he tried! One time at school, he broke into the basketball court so he could play. He had climbed through the window to get inside. Afterward, his conscience ate at him, and he turned himself in.

Butch hated dishonesty and had a zealousness for justice. He was a man who walked with integrity and an upright heart. If he thought someone was being ripped off, he did something about it. He couldn't sit back and watch people be taken advantage of.

Once, an older lady hired him to install an alarm system for her home. In doing so, he realized how poorly her house had been wired and thought she was at risk of an electrical fire. God miraculously provided all new wires, and Butch completely rewired her home in exchange for a good bowl of soup and conversation. He said he had to do it. Otherwise, he would not have been able to sleep. It was always such a joy for him to set his hands to noble tasks.

My sister TK often wondered if Butch was real. She said he was like an angel. He always seemed to be at the right place at the right time to help someone, and people always saw his sincerity. He believed in looking out for those who needed help and would show God's love to them in very practical ways.

Butch was a handyman who would fix anything—from irons to cars to anything that needed fixing. The kids and their friends constantly watched him at work. One night in the barn, one of our friend's children stood up and said, "Uncle Butch, we need prayer." The child believed Uncle Butch could fix anything. "My mom said she's going to leave us, and I'm scared, Uncle Butch."

Butch was able to pray not only for the young child, helping to remove the fear in that moment, but he was able to reach out to the parents and help save their marriage. He appointed himself as an accountability partner to this family, and they were grateful for Butch's loving wisdom, friend-ship, and counsel.

Butch helped many men start their own businesses. He would sit them down, tell them what it would take to a run a company, and help practically where he could. He often worked overtime, helping people build their own places. I remember one particular man had been trying to finish his barn for ten years. Butch decided this had been going on long enough and helped him finish it.

So many young men loved to hang around Butch. He was a father figure to so many. Our dear friend Doug told me af-ter Butch died that he had always wanted a dad to show him how to work with tools. Butch was always so willing to take these young men under his wing, but I know it was so much more than just building and fixing cars and houses. Butch had a gift of building and fixing young men's lives and knew how to reach out to them on a practical level.

Chapter 6

Beginning a Family

After my experience as a fifteen-year-old who narrowly escaped having all her female organs removed, becoming pregnant was an absolute miracle from God.

On April 16, 1978, Guiseppe Domiano Michael Gial Lombardo III was born. Right from his birth, Butch and I knew Guiseppe was a special boy. We knew God had an amazing plan for his life because the devil tried to take him out early.

In 1980, something discovered during a routine doctor visit prompted the doctor to have us take Guiseppe to the hospital. He had blue lips and a slightly runny nose. The doctors at Children's Mercy Hospital discovered he had a heart problem. So at the tender age of twenty-one months, Guiseppe was unexpectedly admitted to the hospital.

Over the next seven days, his heart stopped multiple times, but the doctors resuscitated him. They couldn't pinpoint the cause of the problem. Finally, he stabilized. After about a week of Guiseppe, Butch, and me not sleeping with constant checks by medical staff, the doctors determined Guiseppe could finally be discharged the next day. After we got the good news, I urged Butch to go home and rest until he finally gave in.

After a little while I stepped outside Guiseppe's room, leaning against the door to get a minute of fresh air. I heard "code blue" being called out over the intercom. I looked around trying to figure out where all the doctors and nurses were heading. As I watched, I realized they were heading right toward his room! His nurse had gone in to check on him and called the code blue. I watched as the doctors and nurses attempted to revive my son. As I prayed, I felt the guilt of sending Butch home. The medical staff labored to revive Guiseppe, but nothing seemed to be working. I was standing outside the glass window looking into the room when I got a call from the nurse's station saying my husband was on the phone.

"Dear, the enemy tried to hit me on the way home and said he was going to kill my son." Butch had pulled over to a phone booth to call me. "We're not going to agree with death, we are going to speak life, not death."

We prayed and prayed until all of a sudden, I managed to say, "Butch, code blue just happened. I'm outside Guiseppe's room watching it." We hung up, and Butch immediately came back to the hospital.

About fifteen minutes had passed since they called the code blue. Butch came in as the nurses slowly began to unplug Guiseppe's IVs and all the equipment around his bed. They pulled a cover over him, turned to Butch and me, and announced, "I'm sorry, he didn't make it."

In that moment, we did not begin to pray some big theological prayer. The only thing we knew to do was to call on the name above all names. "Jesus!" we cried. "Jesus!"

As we cried out in desperation, we watched God bring life back to our son. We watched as our lifeless son suddenly gasped for air. He was alive! **That's my God!**

You can imagine the pandemonium that broke out in the hospital that day! Baby boy comes back to life after momma calls out the name of Jesus—what an amazing testimony to those people in the hospital. It left most of the doctors and nurses in a state of shock.

After the hospital staff examined Guiseppe and confirmed he was doing fine, they allowed Butch and me to spend about fifteen minutes alone in the room with him. We were able to hold him. As we held our miracle baby, we couldn't help but praise God and thank Him for saving our son.

A reporter came from the *Kansas City Star* to interview us the next day and asked Guiseppe if he was the little boy who had died, and he replied, "No, I'm the little boy that saw Jesus." Giuseppe had an extraordinary vocabulary for a twenty-one month old baby. The photographer took his picture. The reporter wrote the story. But the *Kansas City Star* wouldn't publish it. They sent me the story and the picture, an 8x10 glossy.

Guiseppe stayed in the hospital for several days. Seeing what God had done with him ignited something in our hearts to pray for the sick. We were on the pediatric intensive care floor where lights flashing above the door indicated a code blue, and children died every day.

"This is not just about Guiseppe while you're here. You're here so I can teach you how I work through you," God told me.

During the time Guiseppe remained in the hospital, the Holy Spirit taught me about operating in the Spirit. I was His student, asking Him to show me what He was doing. I walked around and prayed for all the children. The Holy Spirit told me what was going on in the children's homes so I knew how to pray for them. As I walked around praying for the children, I learned to hear God's voice more clearly.

I learned best this way and God knew it. It was all about His glory. What you think is your worst moment is your biggest moment to lean on Him. He gives you opportunity to grow.

Antonino Michael Vincento Gial Lombardo (a.k.a Nino)

Eighteen months after Guiseppe was born, I gave birth to our second son, Antonino Michael Vincento Gial Lombardo, Nino for short. He was creative, artistic, multi-lingual (he spoke many languages), an anointed worship leader, and gifted in so many unusual ways. He was also extremely funny. He could make the whole room laugh and come alive. In fact, things that shouldn't have been fun were fun with him. He was Mr. Popular and loved by all.

Everything was an instrument to Nino and most everything had a sound. He would discover the different pitches in everyday objects and make music in the most innovative and unusual ways. One time he was determined to show me he could play Mozart on his face. Yes, you heard me. He was convinced he could perfectly play a Mozart piece, using his face as a percussion instrument. He used to make up songs for everyone's birthday.

Oh and how he loved food! He was famous for the "Nino sandwich"—five different meats, three cheeses, my own sauce, herbs, spices, fresh lettuce, and kosher pickles.

When Nino was just two years old, I taught him how to bake biscuits. I wanted him to learn to do one thing well to build his inner confidence. Over a two-year period I taught him one step of the recipe at a time, and to do that one well, and then we would move onto the next step. I started by teaching him how to make the dough, use the right ingredients and the proper tools. I gave Nino his own measuring utensils just for his use. It was about the confidence he received from learning to operate in the kitchen. Nino baking was completely normal for us, but I took it for granted, thinking that every family did the same.

One day when my parents were visiting, my father told me Nino claimed to have made the biscuits for breakfast.

"That's right, Daddy. He's been doing it for two years."

"Are you telling me he makes these biscuits himself?" Daddy asked for confirmation.

"Yes, Daddy."

My father had to see his grandson create these wonderful biscuits the next morning. He wasn't in disbelief at my words or in my son's abilities, but he was in awe that I would think to teach him something that was a big undertaking for an itty-bitty guy. The next day my dad got out the camera to tape Nino making the morning biscuits. It made Nino feel important and confident and gave him power as a man. It wasn't about the cooking, but rather that he was able to do things that others couldn't do, especially at his age. At four years old he had total command over the kitchen.

Nino had an eternal focus and led many souls to Christ. Even as a boy, he would witness to anyone and everyone he would come across. He was a magnet to other boys from a very young age. He was larger than life, so secure, and strong. There was just something about Nino that drew people to him, and we recognized this was something God had placed in him to win hearts over to Christ.

Nino made living for Christ something people really wanted to do.

Nino's Angels

In the month before he died, Nino kept seeing angels coming

through his bedroom wall. He told me he was experiencing so much angelic activity—it was as though God was preparing him in a way I can only understand now. There were two particular angels he saw every night, and these were the ones he drew in his notes while in class. It was in this angelic atmosphere that he wrote so many worship songs. I knew my son always loved to write worship songs, but this was different. Something seemed to have accelerated in the Spirit. In fact, one night he wrote twenty-two worship songs in forty-five minutes after waking up at midnight. He wrote them, went back to sleep, and didn't even get to play them for two weeks because he was so busy.

I know my Nino is more alive now than ever before because he resides in the heavenlies. I believe he fulfilled everything he was to do here. Death, where is your sting?... Thanks be to God who always leads us in triumph! (See 1 Corinthians 15:55-57.)

Chapter 7

Butch, the Father

Butch taught his sons to love God with all their hearts. The things of the world did not matter, but he taught the boys to passionately pursue the things that mattered to God. God loves the widows and orphans, and Butch taught his sons to do the same.

As a father, he prayed and asked God to teach him how to be a good dad who would be there for his sons. He knew every dad had the challenge of working hard to provide and coming home exhausted to his family. He prayed every day on his way home from work, "Please, God, lift this exhaustion from me, and teach me how to play with my sons. I want to have energy to play with my boys."

Every night we went out for a walk after dinner as a family. Butch spent time building things with them, playing games with them, and intentionally and actively engaging with them before bedtime. He read and sang to them every night before they fell asleep, so the last thing they thought about was how loved they were by God and their parents.

He took being a dad very seriously. Next to being the best husband he could be, fatherhood was his highest calling. He spent time researching childhood development and trends to see what his sons needed at various stages of their growth, and how he, as a dad, with the help of the Holy Spirit, could develop them to the very best of their potential. A couple of the books that helped him tremendously were *Dare to Discipline* by James Dobson and *The Father's Almanac* by S. Adams Sullivan.

Butch poured his life into Guiseppe and Nino and taught them everything he knew. His desire was that they would go farther and higher in life than he ever did. Raising sons to do even greater things than you is a godly dream every father is blessed to embrace.

Butch was extremely watchful over his boys. He wanted to develop their sense of adventure and freedom within safe boundaries—much like what our heavenly Father does with us. One time we were camping out in the mountains at Big Bear, California. The ranger came over to us and told us there was a bear cub on the loose away from its mother. As Butch was listening to the man telling us about the bear cub, he spotted the cub running across the campsite with our youngest son, Nino, who was five years old at the time, in hot pursuit. Butch ran after him and managed to snag him by the dungarees before he could get too close. Nino was so excited! "Dad, Dad! Look what I got! Can I take it home, Dad?"

Butch didn't want to completely deflate Nino's sense of accomplishment, so he wisely replied, "Son, that's a baby bear, and it's got a momma in the area that could tear you up." They spent the rest of the day catching lizards instead.

Butch was always looking for creative ways to teach his sons to use their own minds without constantly having to be reminded of things or being forced to do things. He made these charts and graphs for everyday kinds of chores or activities the boys needed to learn. There were little stick figures washing their faces, brushing their teeth, putting on clothes, putting the clothes away, and all kinds of other scenarios, which would help remind the boys through pictures and not by us having to nag all the time. Butch wanted his boys to feel excellent, as though they could make up their own minds to do these things and feel proud. Guiseppe, the responsible firstborn, always checked his activities off, but Nino often forget. Every night as a part of bedtime, Butch had little stars he stuck on the charts as a reward for remembering to do these things.

They also had dress charts where Butch gave them the freedom to choose whatever they wanted to wear ninety percent of the time, but for the remaining ten percent, it was agreed that Mom and Dad could help select their outfits or overrule their selection. We usually only applied our veto power when they were getting dressed up for church or going out somewhere special with Mom and Dad.

Because of these type of arrangements, the guys were so secure in who they were and their decision-making abilities. Butch tried wherever he could to train his sons to think for themselves, to make their own decisions, and to be strong-minded in life. Weak-minded men are those who have not had a strong father figure present, teaching them the Word of God and training them in these little things. Ephesians 6:4 (KJV) says, "And, ye fathers, provoke not your children to wrath: but bring them up in the nurture and admonition of the Lord." This verse is often misunderstood as meaning that fathers should not create anger in their children through discipline. But this verse is really saying don't anger your children by *not* teaching them in the ways of the Lord. Imagine the frustration a man has when he realizes later in life that his father did not equip him to stand as a man of God when things come against him. My sons learned real manhood from their father—to be strong-minded leaders, confident in their God-given identity.

Naturally, being the handyman Butch was, he taught his sons many practical skills. He knew how important it was to fine-tune the boys' motor skills before the age of eight. He taught them how to use a drill and to work with other similar equipment. The boys had their own toy tool kits when they were young. Every time something needed fixing, he had the boys come and help him. They copied everything their dad did and they learned incredibly quickly.

When the boys grew older, their toy tool kits got exchanged for the real thing, and they could literally fix anything. Butch would take them out and find stuff that people had thrown away as trash. They would pick up broken, useless junk and fix it up so excellently that they were able to sell it again for cash. My sons eventually put themselves through a private Christian academy, were able to buy their first car with cash, and had their own clothing allowance with the money they made fixing old junk. People were amazed at the skills Guiseppe and Nino had—all taught by their father.

When it came to studying the Word, the boys wanted Butch to teach them just like his students in Bible college—not the stuff they learned in Sunday School. Butch had a real gift of making the Word so practical. He was able to break it open for the boys and help them understand its application on a very practical and down-to-earth manner. I believe this is why our sons were always so quick to respond to the Word. Butch, with his practical wisdom, made it easy for them.

Lessons in Manhood 1986

While living in Huntington Beach, California, my husband made a decision that our sons should understand how money flows in and out of a household. He had old checkbooks he never threw away from where we had lived before. When Guiseppe was about eight years old, Butch crossed out his name and put Guiseppe's name on one checkbook and Nino's on another. Butch had read a book on how much it cost to raise a child annually and monthly, so he wrote this amount in each of the checkbooks for Nino and Guiseppe. Every time they bought a shirt, went out to dinner, bought groceries, or went to a doctor appointment, Butch had them get their checkbooks and help them write and balance their checks.

They filled out their fake check with great self-confidence as it made them feel like they were taking care of themselves and being good stewards of their money. Butch was forever pouring these kinds of principles into his sons.

He kept the checks our sons thought were real in a Ziploc bag and eventually showed them the checks years later. They were so grateful because they noticed other men had not been raised to watch over their money as good stewards and their households suffered for it. By the time they were teenagers, we set up real checking accounts for them because they insisted on paying with their own checks.

One time we went to the dentist when they were seven and eight years old. After the exam, the dentist told them both they needed braces. He had said they needed braces a couple of times and went to get the paperwork. While we waited, I asked Guiseppe if he thought he needed braces. He checked in the mirror and said, "Nope, I don't think so."

"I don't think so either, honey. Maybe after all your adult teeth come in we can look again."

"Mom, I have a funny feeling about the doctor's advice."

"That is the Holy Spirit speaking to you, son," I said. It was about affirming our sons and giving them confidence in their decisions at an early age.

Nino had just started losing his baby teeth. The doctor came back in and told us how much the braces would cost.

"Well, I've been looking at my smile and I think it's pretty good," Guiseppe said. "I don't think I need braces. How about you, Nino?"

I stood by, validating my son with a confident and encouraging look. The doctor looked at me. Nino looked in the mirror and said, "I don't think so, either."

"Are you going to allow them to ignore my advice?"

"They pay their own bills," I told him, and we walked out. At home, I informed Butch privately of everything that had happened so he would be in the know. He called the boys in one at a time for business, and told them to bring their checkbooks. While Nino played in the other room, Guiseppe came in. "How was the dentist appointment? How much did you have to pay? What did the dentist say?" Butch asked.

"He said I needed braces."

"Really? What do you think, son?" Again, he was reinforcing our son to think and form his own opinions so he could confidently make decisions later in life.

"I've been looking at my smile, and I wiggled every tooth, and I think they're good."

"Well, I think they're good, too, son," Butch confirmed. "We will have another dentist check you later in life."

We later learned about dentists pulling scams, putting braces on six- to eight-year-olds before their adult teeth came in.

To further help our sons learn to manage money, Butch gave them quarters for the swap meet. They were allowed to buy whatever they wanted, junk or not. If they wanted something good, they would have to save for it.

Butch often told Nino, "You can go ahead and buy that ten-cent toy, but it will probably break before we get home." And it always did. Nino always bought some cheap plastic thing. Guiseppe had the fine eye and came home with the coolest things because he would save up his quarters and negotiate. If initially turned down, he would go back and make an offer. If he saw something he wanted, he was not afraid to go in at the end of the day, knowing the sellers wouldn't want to haul it back to their vehicle, and offer them fifty cents. If he had a dollar saved up, he would never offer the whole thing; he would work his way up to it.

Butch wanted our sons to discern and learn what is worth buying and what isn't. Guiseppe received the knowledge and weighed things immediately, but it took Nino a year of broken toys to learn. It didn't involve any of our emotions, just our counsel. We didn't make Nino feel bad for the junk he bought; we made him aware. We would say, "Son, did you enjoy playing with that?"

"Yeah!"

"I'm sure they make it sturdier. We'll just have to look."

Gentlemen

We chose to give the boys opportunity to make decisions of their own and to speak manhood into them while they were still young. Most of the time I called them "gentlemen." I knew they would be what I called out.

Once, at a restaurant, Guiseppe put in Nino's and my order. We had ordered and eaten, and when it was time for the bill, the waitress handed me the bill.

"I'll take that, thank you," Guiseppe said. He was eight years old. The waitress looked at him. I honored him as the man at the table. If you treat him like a boy, he will remain a boy. He paid the bill, the tip, and gratefully thanked the waitress, who was stunned at the eight-year-old boy who could handle a situation like this.

Do you know what it does to a boy to put him in a place of authority? It gives him confidence. Imagine what it does for his social skills to know how to look a waitress in the eye and say, "My mother would like a BLT, mayonnaise on the side, with ice tea and no sugar." Butch would hand Guiseppe $25 in the morning and tell him, "Take your mom out to lunch today. Find out what she wants and order it. Then pay for it with this." He always set Guiseppe up for success by telling him approximately what it would cost and what tip to leave.

There were times when I could see the waitress was not respecting or listening to Guiseppe, so when it came time to pay the bill I told him, "I'm going to leave so she can see you're the boss, and you can pay the bill." Nino came with me, acting like my bodyguard at seven years old, and then the waitress would have an *aha* moment and get that this man was going to pay the bill. We frequented the same restaurants so the staff learned how to treat us and how my sons were being raised. God did not call me to raise kids—he called me to raise kings—to give them authority in the world they lived in by walking in grace, kindness, and confidence.

When the boys were little guys, I felt the Lord show me they should be able to have conversations with their father at a bigger level. I had noticed in Bible college that most of the men had broken relationships with their fathers. They were making statements like, "I can't go to my dad with this," and that always stuck in my heart. I wanted my boys to come to dinner at night and feel comfortable presenting anything one-on-one with their dad. When they were five and six years old, the Holy Spirit showed me it was the time of life to start developing that skill.

Every morning I took an article out of a Christian magazine that came to our house in doubles. I would outline one story and give it to Butch with, "This is Nino's" at the top half. At the bottom half of the story I would write "This is Guiseppe's." Then I would go in and wake Nino and read him his section a couple of times so he really got it. I would then take Guiseppe aside in the morning and go over and over his half of the story. By the time they made it to the breakfast table both of them were anxiously waiting for Dad to bring up the topic of the day, which was always the Word of God and how it applies to the way we live now.

Butch would ask Nino a question about his half of the story, which Guiseppe couldn't answer because he didn't know that part. Guiseppe sat patiently, yet excitedly, waiting to hear his questions because he knew he had the rest of the story. The conversations developed an ability in the boys to sit with their father at the table and speak one-on-one, man-to-man. These mature, godly conversations then became normal throughout their whole lives.

As a mother, I don't believe I could be more pleased with how they matured over the years. They weren't perfect, but they were mine, and I was so proud of them. They walked a life of repentance and forgiveness. They were both Bible college students, men of integrity, and loved serving their community. They were always eager to stop and help someone in need.

I remember going to the bank one day to make a deposit and the teller said, "Mrs. Lombardo, I broke down on the highway this morning, and your two sons got out of their car and came walking toward me." She told me she was scared at first because it was dark, and she couldn't tell who had stopped. She was relieved when the boys yelled out they were the Lombardo brothers and asked if they could help. The teller told me, "That was such a sweet moment because I knew I was safe." The boys were unable to fix her car, but they drove her to work and had the car towed. Acts of kindness were not unusual for them.

Guiseppe and Nino lived their lives in an effort to love others, bring glory to God, and bring souls to Christ.

Chapter 8

Tent Stories

One night in early 1983, I had a dream.

"Honey, the Lord just showed me something." I told Butch the whole dream.

"Stop." Butch was a melancholy personality, very detailed. He pulled out a legal pad to take notes.

"I saw us moving to California. My vision was drawn on graph paper. I saw us moving to a mountain pass and living in a tent. Then we moved to a busier part of California by the ocean. I saw the amount of money you would make when you start your own company. Then we moved back to Kansas. We live in a house that has two front doors, a tiny bay window, a bedroom over the garage, and we're on a lot of land. I saw you making a certain amount of money when we moved into that house."

"How much land was there? I don't want a lot of land."

"It's not five acres; it's not two." It turned out to be almost three acres. "We're sleeping over the garage, and we have three bedrooms and two baths. There's a deck on the back." I described the house God showed me.

"Why are you happy about this? I don't want to live in a tent. We're *not* moving to California. No, we're not going there," he said.

Within a few months of my having that dream, an alarm systems company in California offered Butch a job as a troubleshooter. The offer was incredible, with great opportunities for him, and the money looked fantastic. Part of the deal included a house. In fact, the company pre-walked us through this enormous house—four bedrooms and three bathrooms. It was beautiful and everything we had hoped for.

I called my sisters immediately and described the house in detail. "You won't believe this house," I exclaimed. We were all excited about our new home. TK, who lived in Albuquerque, New Mexico, told me she was coming to spend her first vacation with us in our new house, along with her husband and two children, Gabriel and Angel.

Within three weeks of the offer, we sold the furniture, loaded the trailer, and headed to the house in Monterey.

Things got interesting at our first meeting with my husband's new company. As I've said, they made us this unbelievable offer and told us, "The money is here! This is where you want to be! We want you!" But when we walked into the meeting with them, after we had accepted the offer, they looked at us and said, "We lied about the house."

"Oh," I said, "I saw it wasn't completely ready when you walked us through. Is it not done yet?"

"No, it wasn't even ours to show you," they replied.

"You mean, it wasn't your house to show us?" I asked, a little confused.

"That's right. And it's not your house either. In Monterey, only one percent of the market is rental, and there are no houses for sale."

I was shocked. We both were. The man who hired Butch brought us to Monterey under false pretenses. Now he was telling us we didn't have a house and would not be able to rent one either. He went on to explain that due to the picking season, all the illegal aliens had moved in—rumor was seventeen people to a hotel room—and occupied what little rental space there was. Being from the Midwest, when I heard the term "illegal aliens," all I could think of was beings from outer space.

They also told us all the hotels were fully booked.

They explained migrant workers from Mexico had come to look for work during the picking season, picking all the different kinds of fruit from the orchards, as well as spices for an American spice company.

"Oh!" I said. "Mexicans. Why didn't you just say so?"

There we were, having driven all the way from Kansas City, Missouri, to Monterey, California, and we had nowhere to live. Nino was three and one-half and Guiseppe almost five.

"Honey, we passed a campground on the way here, about sixty miles out of town. It had a merry-go-round, a park with animals, and looked really cute. Couldn't we put up our tent and give the boys a fun night?" We had been driving solid for three days, which is a lot of driving with two small boys in the back seat. It's 1,616 miles from Kansas City to Los Angeles, and Monterey was a further six-hour drive north.

So that's what we did. We thought it would only be for one night until we figured out something else. On April 1, we pulled into site 136A and managed to get our little two-man pup tent set up for the night. My mom had given us a fluorescent orange tent for Christmas, and we were also given a cooler, a stove, a lantern, and sleeping bags for the four of us. This would be fun! A cute little night out with the boys in our tent before we hit the town the following day to call as many real estate agents as we could to find something else. Or so we thought.

All the Realtors said the same thing: There is absolutely nothing available. We looked farther and farther out from Monterey, but we were told the same thing. Nothing would be available until the picking season ended. Everyone told us to call back in October or November! We kept trying and trying, all the while staying in our little tent, which very soon became our "home sweet home." It was hard for a moment, but we knew God had called us to move here. It wasn't about the job, it wasn't about the house, it was about the location God called us to.

Meanwhile, my husband slept on the ground with the three of us snuggled around him in our little tent. He got up at 3:30 every morning and went to the coffee shop to put on his suit and tie for his very important job. He had to get up that early so he wouldn't be late, and I knew he wouldn't be home much before 7:30 p.m. The boys and I stayed behind at the campground.

The first day he pulled out to go to work, the boys and I stood there trying to look like the perfect little picture. I wore a skirt that went all the way down to my ankles and my huarache sandals. I had two little boys holding onto my skirt, all of us trying to look happy for Dad as he pulled off and looked back at us in the rear view mirror. I told the boys to keep smiling because I knew it would be hard for Butch to leave us all behind. He had such a father's heart.

As he pulled away, I remember thinking, Oh God, is he coming back? Because it was a confusing route from Monterey to the campground. For a brief moment in my head, I saw we were living in a tent, with no bathroom, no sink, and I didn't know where we were. I wanted to cry, but I kept those feelings inside because I wanted my sons to see "more than a conqueror," like in Romans 8:37 (KJV) where the apostle Paul says, "Nay, in all these things we are more than conquerors through Him who loved us." It was so important I create a positive atmosphere for my boys. I would not give the enemy a foothold for fear or negativity.

Our home became that little campground in that California mountain pass. It turned out we were the fifth family that same company lied to. The others families were all living in small trailers in different areas.

I cooked on a camp stove, but mostly we gathered wood, and I cooked over an open fire. It was two months before Butch received his first paycheck, which put us into a real bind. Yet, challenging as it was, I was truly happy. To have my family together, seeing what God had planned for us in such an amazingly beautiful place, made it feel like I was in the Garden of Eden.

Things started happening right away. God brought all sorts of beautiful people into our lives during those tent days, and He had a plan for each one of them.

On my first afternoon of living in the tent, I was busy putting the boys to sleep for a nap. I laid a blanket down, and I sat there with their heads on my lap. I had my Bible out and was singing the words of the Bible in a soothing tone to get them to sleep. A woman came across to where we were sitting, took a look at my Bible, and asked if I was a Christian. When I answered yes, she said she had a biblical question to ask me—a question that had been worrying her for a long time. I was able to break open the Scriptures for her and point her to the truth.

Little did I know that my years in Bible college would be used sitting in the tent! This was the beginning of something amazing God was doing, and there were so many people who came to us after her, people whose lives would be changed and impacted with the Word of God. Just because we were living in that tent. God brought them to us.

I taught the boys the Word of God and told them stories from the Bible. All the while I didn't realize people could hear me and were gathered round the tent to listen to the Word. I taught the boys that these stories in the Bible weren't just stories, but they were the legacy and heritage of our family. We fully embraced the "brothers and sisters in Christ" by viewing King David and the other Israelites as our family ancestors.

I sang to the boys at night, and people would listen to the songs as I was singing and join in. You know, when your home is a tent, I guess it's pretty easy for people to hear everything you're saying. At the time, I didn't realize people could hear me. It was my home, and this is how we lived. But those thin tent walls allowed people to hear the truth, and they were drawn to God.

One woman in particular, who was on drugs at the time, came into the tent as I was telling the story of Noah. I asked Guiseppe to explain it. She was mesmerized by this five-year-old boy speaking words of life to her heart.

Many came and sat with us as I taught the Word to my sons and would ask if they could learn the Word from me. These people were primarily pickers—those illegal aliens I mentioned earlier—who came with their Bibles, hungry to learn. Whenever I taught the Word, I often asked people for their Bibles before we began. I would flip to the page we would be studying so if people didn't know where it was, Satan would not be able to bring confusion as they hunted for the passage. Showing them the verse usually made people feel more at ease, and they were more open to the Word.

On one particular occasion, I took the man's Bible and was flipping through it. As I was thumbing through the pages—page after page—I thought, What is going on? Why can't I find this passage? I closed his Bible and prayed, thinking to myself that this was most definitely a spirit of confusion at work. As I prayed, the Lord said to me, "Look at it again, Cindi." I looked at the Bible, and then at the man. "Wait a minute! Does this say Mateo, Marcos, Lucas, Juan?"

He nodded.

"So this book is all in Spanish?"

He nodded again.

"Ok!" I chuckled to myself. "Let's go to Juan tres." I flipped to John 3. And yes, we went to verse sixteen.

People often came to me at night wanting to have a Bible study. Our campsite was situated in a mountain pass, which made it extremely dark, so I would tell people to bring their flashlights. We sat in the pitch dark, with our flashlights right on our heads, looking down at our Bibles. God had me teach this way, but only after Butch and the boys were sound asleep. Butch had to go to sleep very early because he needed to be up early in the morning to make the two-hour drive to work.

People came from all over. That little lady who had the biblical question that had been bothering her—well, she packed up her pop-up trailer that same day and just left. She came back the following day with three other trailers following her. She had left to fetch her sons and their families, and they had come to listen to this "tent lady" share the Word of God. I sat and taught them under the tree, just like I would teach my own sons, and she knew her sons were to come and listen.

Other church people also came and listened. Mormons, Catholics, and Baptists all came wanting to learn. People who had never heard the Word of God came to hear. Stories of the Tent Lady started to spread farther and farther as people's lives were impacted with the Word of God.

People streamed in. I actually had to put a sign up on the tree that read, *Please Do Not Disturb*, unless my sons were napping, otherwise people would have come in all the time, and I did not want to lose my time with my sons. My first call was to raise up my sons in the Word. They were my first responsibility, and I would not lose sight of it. My time with them would not be stolen.

People will always come and go—Jesus said the poor and needy would always be among us. You need to recognize when you have to restore and build up your own home first, and then you will always have the opportunity to tend to the needy. God is faithful to give you the avenues to do so, but family comes first. Otherwise, the phone will never stop ringing—it never stopped ringing even when we moved into our own apartment. The needs never stopped, they never became less, but we never lacked fellowship as a family because we set up the necessary boundaries. The boundaries were simple: Don't talk to me when my sons are awake. We told people when my sons' nap times were and said they could visit during those hours.

So the people could come during naptime; otherwise I would not get my time with my family. I realized it was a mom who raised presidents, and a mom who raised kings. Satan would do anything to take me away from my sons. Satan was the thief in John 10:10 coming to steal time that could not be replaced.

Above all the other days in the tent, June 25, 1983, my seventh wedding anniversary, stands out in my memory. We had been living in the tent for three months exactly. The traffic on the road coming into where we stayed was completely backed up for miles. The traffic was so heavy that police officers had been sent in to figure out what was causing the problem.

A police officer came up to me at the tent and asked, "Are you the Tent Lady?"

You can imagine my surprise. I wasn't sure if it was a question or an accusation. He took out a saddlebag and dumped a big heap of cards and letters on a picnic table beside our tent and asked me, "Ma'am, can I ask you what it is that you're selling at this tent?"

You see, so many people had been saved in those three months, and they had all asked when our anniversary was. They wanted to send us cards to congratulate us.

"I'm not selling anything."

"No? Ma'am, we've gotten letters from car to car," he said, pointing to the traffic piled up. He reached for one of the letters to open it.

"Don't you open that without me praying first!" I shouted. You can imagine his reaction of shock and puzzlement.

"Excuse me, ma'am?" he questioned authoritatively.

So I prayed. "Father God, I am sensing this letter is a need, so, Lord, before this man opens it, may You just answer the needs that are in these letters."

The policeman looked at me strangely and then opened the letter. Sure enough, it was a prayer request. He opened another, and all it said was "Happy Anniversary!"

"What are you telling these people, ma'am?" The officer was genuinely confused, and I could tell he was having trouble understanding what was happening.

"I'm not telling them anything, except that Jesus Christ is Lord and Savior," I answered.

"Well, get him out here!" he said, thinking I was referring to a person in the tent.

I picked up my Bible, showing it to him. "As in Jesus Christ. He is that real to me."

The police officer gave his life to the Lord right then and there. He told me what the owner of the campground had said to him that ever since we moved in, the campground had overflowed with people. The owner told the officer that before we moved in, they were on the brink of bankruptcy. We were like Jacob in Genesis 30 and 31—no matter where God put Jacob, the land was blessed.

Now, my husband wasn't home—he was stuck in the traffic. He couldn't imagine what was going on that the traffic was backed up so badly. When he found out it was me, he said, "Dear, I guess if you're a child of the King you can't be hidden anywhere. I could put you in a tent in the middle of nowhere, and they're gonna search the world over to find you!"

What a way to celebrate your seventh anniversary! I have a beautiful letter from my husband from that day in the tent. He was crazy about me. He understood we had what people needed—the love of God, which could never be contained or restricted to our tent. God's love was like a magnet, drawing people in from all walks of life.

That's my God!

CHAPTER 9

Campground Ministry Continues

Our time at the campground was a Jacob story (see Genesis 29-31). To give you a bit of background, when we went into "Laban's land," the campsite was not doing well at all. The owner, an Italian man by the name of Joe Z, drove around in his Cadillac Eldorado counting the number of heads he could see in the campsite. Since we had been there, the campsite had filled up, but I never understood what he was doing when I heard that diesel engine of his revving every night as he drove past our tent.

"Butch, what is he doing?"

"He's counting his money, dear, making sure the office keeps the money truthful because everyone pays in cash, and it's too easy to miss someone."

This became the ritual every night. "Here he comes, boys!" I'd say when I heard that Cadillac engine.

Joe Z would pull up, roll down the window, and say, "What are you smiling about? Don't you know you live in a tent?"

"It doesn't make a difference to me if it's brick, wood, or canvas—it's not the size of my home, it's the size of my heart that matters."

"Lady, you're living in a tent on the side of the road!" he said, as if that was supposed to make me feel really bad.

"Joe, my whole family is together and we're well and we love God. Is there anything more we could ask for?"

Joe got saved before the summer was over. He had been charging us horrendous amounts of money to live in that tent. We paid more than double the amount we paid years before for our Kansas house.

Some people streaming into the campground and renting sites near us in order to see the Tent Lady were millionaires. They asked Joe how much he was really charging us to live in that tent. After Joe got saved, the Holy Spirit convicted him of the exorbitant fee, and he dropped the rent to nearly one-third of the price. **That's my God!**

Who would have thought God would bring millionaires to rent spaces at our campsite in order to hear the Word of God? You should have seen some of their motor homes—some of them with solid gold sinks.

"Honey, it doesn't make sense that all of these millionaires would come here and rent all these spots. This is a tent! This is a campground!" my husband said.

But God was moving on a Tent Lady, pouring out His love on all kinds of people who really needed it, from Hollywood millionaires, to *Vogue* models, to world-champion tennis players, to restaurant owners, to illegal immigrants from Mexico. We didn't see anyone as any different. There were no levels of people—they were all beautiful to us.

During this time we created many beautiful relationships that are still close to me almost thirty years later. The boys and I walked throughout the campsite singing, and children would follow us. I am so grateful for each one of the beautiful people God added to our family and the joy of their friendship today.

God brought our baby girl, Dara Ann, who saw us at the

campground pool one day. We adopted her in our hearts as our daughter, and she has been a missionary with her husband and children in El Salvador. Whenever I hear the songs "Purify My Heart" or "Sanctuary," I am reminded of my baby girl from the tent. Dara Ann would sing these songs to me, years after the tent when my sons were in their high school years. No matter who sings them now, in my heart it is always Dara singing to me.

One day we found a six-month-old baby at the door of the tent with a note that said, "I have been watching you, and you would be a better mother than me." God revealed to me the mother of the baby was trying to kill herself, and I told that to Guiseppe and Nino. I never hid things like this from my sons. My response determined their destiny. I taught them the truth in order to raise them up as strong men of God who understood the enemy's scheme. We believed in a strong God. I knew He wanted to save this family, and I wanted my sons to witness the miracle.

We took a walk with the baby, up and down a mountain slope and down toward the river. We saw a lady lying flat on her face in the water, so I quickly handed the baby to Guiseppe and went to her. The mother rose up toward us. She was frothing at the mouth, demonically possessed. I had never experienced a demonic manifestation before. The Holy Spirit told me to put out my hand and proclaim the name of Jesus. I obeyed.

The lady dropped to the ground and rose up again. She did this three times in total. I hadn't yet learned that sometimes you have to pray more than once for a full deliverance to happen. I was just being led by the Holy Spirit. I later found out this lady had been addicted to cocaine from the age of thirteen until she was twenty-seven or twenty-eight.

God dried her out and freed her from her addiction. I helped take care of her, and after about six weeks she disappeared.

A couple of weeks later, a very expensive car pulled up, and a gorgeous, refined woman stepped out and began calling my name. "Cindi Lombardo?"

"Yes, that's me," I replied, still unsure of who she was. She was the drug addict whom we had taken in and who had disappeared with her baby after six weeks. She was wealthy and living in Monterey, having been a cocaine supplier to those in the area. She said she had never had anyone take her in and give her their everything. She told me there was a whole group of people in Monterey who were mad at me and wanted to beat me up because I had dried up their supplier. All I could think to say was, "Please bring them down here." So they came and rented the spot right next to us to try to do something to us that would turn their supplier back.

I warned my sons the Holy Spirit had told me a lady would come, approach me, and slap me with all she had, but that it would be okay because I wasn't really going to feel anything. It was important they knew their momma was going to be okay. And then it happened that day. A lady walked angrily up to me and slapped me with everything she had. Both of my sons stood confidently beside me, knowing I was alright.

I stood there. "You can hit me all you want, but God is still real. He still sent His only Son to die for you."

She stared at me for a moment, then broke down crying, and received Christ.

On July 4, a family gave us a brand new 8x10 foot tent they had bought but never used because they got a trailer instead. We felt like we'd moved into the Hilton with all that space!

"Do you know—"

"Don't say how many more people we can take in," Butch interrupted me. When God gives you more space, He gives you more people to take care of. Between seven and eight people would live in that tent at one time. As I said before, it's not the size of your home, but the size of your heart that matters. I knew our time in this tent was "but a season" and God would give me what we needed every step of the way. Our season there became a time of embracing what God was doing and opening our hearts and our home to others. The reason we were able to open up our family to outsiders like this was because my husband and I were in complete agreement, and our hearts were completely wrapped around each other. Our family bond was strong.

My husband often said of those times in the tent that he never knew what he would come home to. Who would be the newest *members* of the family that night? But it was never a strain or a burden for him because the Lord Himself told Butch a child of the King cannot be hidden.

We loved our time in the tent.

Another miracle worth mentioning is that I had prayed and asked the Lord that it wouldn't rain and that there would be no snakes during the time we were there. Sure enough, there was no sign of any snakes, which is highly unusual for that part of the country. California had a drought in 1983, and the very day we left the campground, it started to sprinkle.

Imagine God sending a family to live in a tent to minister to people in unusual areas. He always has a remnant somewhere. Many people were saved in the middle of a mountain range in California. **That's my God!**

I Have a New Friend, Grandmama

Our days in the tent ended after a year, and after a few adventures, we rented an apartment in Huntington Beach, California In 1985, my parents came to visit for their thirtieth wedding anniversary.

Guiseppe was so full of excitement and joy that his grandmama would get to meet his new friend. "Grandmama, I've got a great new friend called Raymond. I can't wait for you to meet him."

"Oh, I look forward to meeting your new friend, Guiseppe," she said politely.

We were sitting having breakfast under an umbrella at a place called The Sugar Shack on the main street of Huntington Beach. My mother spotted a homeless man busy pulling newspapers out of the trash can to wipe his hands with. Giuseppe got all excited, and with horror, she realized this was Guiseppe's new friend.

"Raymond, Raymond, come and meet Grandmama!" Guiseppe shouted.

"Oh no, Cindi, you're not serious," my mother said, surprised. Raymond was not who she had expected as her grandson's friend. She expected a seven-year-old little boy, not a fifty-year-old homeless man digging through the trash.

Raymond grabbed a piece of newspaper out the trash can as you would a wash rag, wiped his hands, and even slicked back his hair as he walked over to introduce himself. "Well, you must be Grandmama! I know it's your thirtieth anniversary; the boys told me. I would shake your hand, but Guiseppe said you like to keep things clean. Congratulations on your anniversary."

Momma was incredibly surprised at how intelligent he was. He gave her the news of the day and the political information of what was going on in her state. She sat there with the rest of us, completely amazed. Raymond was fascinating to listen to. He was really a treat to my parents. After Raymond went on his way, my momma said, "So, tell me about Raymond."

"Oh, Grandmama, he used to be a famous lawyer but lost everything in the divorce. He said his wife took him to the dry cleaners," Guiseppe answered, as only a seven-year-old could tell it.

Later that night, we walked the Huntington Beach Pier, as we did every night.

"Hey, Grandmama, come with me. Trust me," Guiseppe said. She followed, then stopped short.

"Guiseppe, this is the men's restroom!"

But he led her straight into the restroom, walked directly to the last stall, and opened the door. There was Raymond, asleep. Guiseppe had been collecting newspaper out of the trash and had taken it on the walk with him. My mom could see there was purpose in her grandson's face. She watched him cover Raymond with the newspapers and pat him, saying, "It's okay, it's me, Raymond. I just came to cover you up." Then Guiseppe sang a lullaby, our version of "Mary had a little lamb." He patted Raymond again and said, "Goodnight. I love you, Raymond," and then kissed him on the cheek, which was covered in dirt. It was clean to Guiseppe. You see, he understood the reason he was here—to love the brokenhearted.

CHAPTER 10

Back to Kansas

In early 1989, we felt the Lord calling us back to the Kansas City area. We moved into the basement of my parent's house in Lansing, Kansas. It was such a blessing for my parents that we moved in because we were able to help take care of Uncle Timmy. They were finally able to do some traveling around the country. That year was a kiss from God.

Shortly thereafter, we moved into our first apartment in Shawnee, Kansas. Butch went to all of the alarm companies in the area and showed them how he could be the best sub-contractor they would ever hire.

Butch began training the boys how to use the same tools he used. He bought them their own compasses, head lamps, and voice-activated head sets. By the time the boys were ten and twelve, they were on the alarm jobs with Butch. By the time they were seventeen and eighteen years old, they had their own security companies.

He Doesn't See the Wheelchair; He Sees the Person

As a little boy, Guiseppe was used to seeing his Uncle Tim, a quadriplegic, in a wheelchair, so it wasn't a strange or un-comfortable thing for him. One time, we all went to the

Abilities Seminar in St. Louis, Missouri, which profiled the latest in handicap equipment. My parents were there looking for the latest invention to help with Timmy's daily life.

Guiseppe saw a huge painting of a cougar on a rock and for some reason was completely taken with this picture. "Momma, I have to have this picture." This was not at all like him. He never asked for anything. Butch and I taught the boys that God had all their needs and wants covered. We didn't want the kind of children who would be caught up in material things. Even though it was totally out of character for him, he kept at it. "Mom, I have to have this."

He was adamant, and the nuns who were there told us the painting wasn't for sale because it was up for raffle.

"But I have to have it, Momma." Guiseppe was ten years old at the time.

We were told the artist was present at the event and would be making prints available, which we could buy. Guiseppe decided he would wait for the artist to come out, and then he would buy the print from the artist himself. He was deeply drawn to whoever had created that painting.

When someone announced the artist was coming through, people made way for this man in a wheelchair who had no arms. Guiseppe immediately made his way to him and moved to hold him. The man started yelling, "Get him off me!"

"It's okay, it's okay. God loves you," Guiseppe said.

The man stopped yelling, and Guiseppe stood on the peddle of the wheelchair, the same way he would to give my brother a hug. A *real* hug. He began to embrace this man and kiss his cheek, which made the artist feel uncomfortable. "Get off me! Get this kid off me!" he shouted.

"No," my son replied. "You'll just have to stand it for a minute; I won't leave you. This is the love of God for you."

Tim, who was there with us, saw this from a distance and came over to help as the artist said, "Aren't you afraid of this wheelchair, kid?"

"He's not a kid; he's my nephew," Tim explained to the man. "He doesn't see your wheelchair. He sees the person." The artist calmed down and let Guiseppe stay there.

He fell in love with Guiseppe—he didn't want him to leave. He wept and Guiseppe wiped away his tears. The artist ended up giving the painting to Guiseppe as a gift. This moment was bigger than my words would ever be able to express. My ten-year-old son loved so deeply that, like God, he saw the heart of the man and not the external form.

Guiseppe's Eyesight

When Guiseppe was thirteen years old, the doctor told us he was going to lose his eyesight. In fact, the doctor said Guiseppe wouldn't just lose his eyesight, but he would go blind quickly. During this time, he got the most terrible migraines and would throw up all the time. We got him glasses. After a week, the glasses wouldn't help him. That's how fast his eyesight was deteriorating.

One night, we were all in the living room studying the Word. Guiseppe was having one of those terrible migraines, and I had put ice on the back of his neck to try and ease the pain. As I sat there, tenderly rubbing his head, he fell asleep on the floor. About that time a group of men arrived at our house. They had come to pray for Guiseppe's eyesight. These men knew God was going to heal my son. We all took hands to pray for Guiseppe, and each of us felt an extreme heat rise up from his body. The heat rose from where he was lying on the floor, and we all knew God had healed him.

While praying for Guiseppe's eyesight to be healed, one of

the men had a vision. He saw Guiseppe in a car accident two weeks before he turned nineteen. He saw the police write DOA (dead on arrival) and that a lot of kids would be affected by his death. This upset me; you never want to hear such a prophecy. I tried to release everyone and say good-bye that night, but it shook my husband and me for years. We continually prayed against the plan of the enemy.

The next morning, Guiseppe came to the table without his glasses. We didn't say anything. The second morning, the same thing happened. On the third morning after the men had prayed for him, Guiseppe said, "Dad, something's happened. God healed me. I heard God say, 'You are healed.'"

We hadn't told Guiseppe about what had happened that night. He was fast asleep when God healed him. We first wanted to hear from Guiseppe that he was healed. We wanted it to come from him so it wouldn't be something we projected onto him.

He never wore his glasses again but kept them as a testimony.

A Boys' Home

In Kansas City there used to be a home for boys between the ages of about two and seventeen years who have no existing relatives. The conditions were extremely sad, and my husband felt strongly that we should get involved as a family. He got permission from the head of the center for our family to go in every Friday night to spend time with the boys.

I remember the first time we went there. Butch said, "Nino, get your guitar, we're going to the boy's home."

Now, my father had warned me what I was going to feel as I walked in because he had been in a boys' home himself. He said before people were due to visit, the boys were given a bar of soap. He told me he used the whole bar of soap to scrub and scrub himself so he would be good and clean enough that someone would pick him. "So when you walk in, sweetheart, you're going to smell the strongest smell of soap you've ever smelled."

And I did. It overwhelmed me. I had to slip into the women's bathroom and weep because I realized they all wanted to be picked. They came in and sat down all around us, with caretakers or guards who came in with them.

Nino started playing his guitar, and we began to worship. Some of the older boys started whispering amongst themselves. They all seemed to be staring at Guiseppe's shoes. Guiseppe had just come from basketball practice, and he had bought himself a brand new pair of shoes. Our sons had to pay for their own sports gear, so Guiseppe had bought these shoes with his own money. In fact, he had discussed this with the team and tried to convince them to get less expensive shoes. Anyway, he had on these expensive shoes, and the older boys were staring at them. Guiseppe started untying his basketball shoes. I watched him do this, wondering what he was doing, but we were still worshiping so I didn't get a chance to ask him until we got into the car that night.

"Guiseppe, what was that all about—untying your tennis shoes?" I said once we were in the car.

"Mom, I was prepared to give them away. I wanted to be ready if God said I should."

When we got home, Guiseppe and Nino went straight to the closet where they had put the new clothes they had bought for the new school year. Some of these clothes still had their price tags on them. Guiseppe started packing them all into a bag and said, "Momma, those boys all had used clothes on. Why do people give used clothes?"

Guiseppe was adamant. "Momma, we have to go back

and help these kids." So, the next Friday night we took the bag of new clothes and shoes the guys had bought with their own money to give to the kids. Guiseppe and Nino were always in that mindset of giving away what they had. We took them to the thrift store to buy clothes with the leftover money in their budget.

So, Friday nights, or Lombardo nights as we called them, became something that went on for years. We went to the center every week so the guys could talk to the boys and show them God's love. It was also an opportunity for the boys in the center to experience the love of a family. We approached several churches that eventually got involved and helped.

Guiseppe and Nino were at their happiest when they were helping people, especially kids.

The Knights

I homeschooled Guiseppe and Nino while we lived in California and continued to homeschool after we moved back to Kansas in 1989. In 1994, we enrolled them in a private Christian school for their high school years.

One night while my sons were in high school, they were home with several buddies watching a movie called *First Knight.* About halfway into it, there was a knock at the front door, and Nino jumped up to get it. We heard a young man's voice say, "Nino, I can't take it anymore. They're beating me up." He knew my family would help in any way they could, and our home was always a place of refuge.

My husband leapt to his feet and so did Guiseppe. While the young man was still at the door, Nino, Guiseppe, and Butch prayed for him. They held this young man and helped bring him into the living room.

Butch then went into a fatherly talk of how important it

was to stick together. He spoke of the options and the ways to handle this and how to look out for one another. "If you all stand for the things of God and help each other and stay faithful to His word, it will make a difference. Just like in Daniel, chapters 1, 2, and 3."

Nino stood and headed downstairs to throw on the Shopsmith. We used the Shopsmith for making things with wood. Butch loved to work with wood and had taught his sons. While Nino was busy downstairs, all the guys went back to watching *First Knight*. As the movie ended, Nino arrived upstairs with twelve wooden swords. He threw them on the floor and announced, "We are now known as the Knights of the Semi-Rectangular Table!" Later he shortened this to "the Knights." It was somewhat of a joke that night, but they had no idea how big this would become. A few buddies with some wooden swords and a lot of heart for one another impacted many lives.

The next day as the boys and their friends made their way into the school lunchroom, they noticed one table had place mats on it with bold lettering. These placemats read "Sir Knight Guiseppe Lombardo," "Sir Knight Nino Lombardo," and so on for each of the knights.

Guiseppe came to me later and said this could be a lot bigger than we realized.

"Yes, son, I think you're right." They all got a big kick out of it, but everyone knew who the Knights were. The boy who was being bullied was never touched again. The Knights were protecting each other physically and spiritually.

Whatever you see in the natural is in the supernatural.

Their friend Peter Freund, who had made the placemats, said he and Nino had started talking in class, which had given him the idea. Guiseppe had already started setting up dinners for the knights at my table—or shall I say, "The Semi-Rectangular Table." Nino drew a logo with the help of Peter and another friend, Levi. It was a sword and shield with the letter *K* bursting through. Nino had the logo embroidered on twelve Italian T-shirts (white tank tops) for the guys. The shirt was one of their first gifts with this emblem. By the time prom came around, Nino had silk handkerchiefs with the emblem made for all the guys, to go with their tuxedos.

Yes, the fun was coming through, but the rules of the Knighthood were being set up. Their dad said they had to help widows and orphans. They were to do secret deeds to help people, and there were plenty of opportunities to do so.

Once, we had an ice storm in early October, completely out of season for our area. The storm devastated the Kansas City area, breaking tree branches all over the city, blocking doors so people couldn't get out of their homes. The branches also brought down a lot of power lines, leaving people stranded in their homes without electricity. They couldn't go out and get food or supplies. The elderly were trapped in bad situations in their homes. When my sons heard this, they went out, got supplies, and with gas-powered chainsaws, helped get the supplies through to those who were stuck.

It was all over the news that some people were going around charging very high fees to help.

Then the news broke, saying, "There are two brothers going in and helping the elderly. We have had calls coming in saying that two guys have been going from door to door leaving groceries on their steps and cutting down the trees in front of their houses at no charge." The only signature they left behind on the doorstep was a *K,* the Knights logo.

"Honey, your sons are on the news," Butch said.

"How do you know it's them? They just said two brothers,

they didn't give their names."

"Look, honey" he said, pointing to the emblem of the Knights on the television screen.

There it was, the blue and silver emblem of the Knights. Even though the news didn't interview them or even show who they were, we knew it was our guys. My sons went from house to house asking if there was a senior citizen or anyone handicapped because they wanted to help those who were not strong enough to help themselves.

My sons were always doing secret deeds, but started leaving the emblem of the Knights wherever they went. People started calling our house, asking if they could get help from the Knights. Guys were asking to be part of the Knights—the very guys you would call the troublemakers in school.

It was apparent to us the Knights were growing.

The Vision

Two weeks before Guiseppe's nineteenth birthday in 1997, the guys went to a party to get the football jerseys for a local flag football team they had joined. They had just left an Easter play at the church and were going to meet us at home. As the guys were leaving the party with one of their football players, they decided to help a friend who had been drinking by taking him home. Nino drove his friend's car while Guiseppe drove ahead of them in his own vehicle. They had just received their jerseys for the football team and were all heading home so they could get some sleep before leaving for their big game together the following day.

They were stopped at a red light, and as the light turned green, Guiseppe pulled into the intersection going straight ahead. Just past the intersection a semitruck made an illegal turn and hit Guiseppe's car on the driver's side, rolling up and over his car. The collision blew out all the tires and windows on Guiseppe's car. The roof was completely caved in and the hood flipped up and off. The semi landed on top of Guiseppe's car. The truck's gas tank had burst and was leaking all over the car. There were tire marks from the semi on the seat Guiseppe was sitting on, as well as over the roof. The truck dragged Guiseppe's car a full seventy-five feet before they came to a halt.

Under God's watchful eye, the car behind Guiseppe was a police car. There was also another police car sitting in a parking lot at the corner where it all happened. Nino, who saw the whole thing happen, raced to the car to try and pull his brother out. By the time he got there, two cops were on either side of Guiseppe's vehicle, and one of them was busy writing DOA on his report.

In the meantime, the friend they were taking home was busy calling Butch and me. Seconds before the phone rang, I heard the Holy Spirit say, "Guiseppe was in a car accident" while it was happening. I was at home getting ready for bed when I saw Guiseppe in a car accident. I got such a shock, and blurted, "Butch, I saw Guiseppe in a car accident!" Butch had just grabbed hold of my hands to pray, when the phone rang. It was the friend calling to tell us what had happened.

"There's an accident! It's Guiseppe! It's Guiseppe!" he yelled at us over the phone.

In the meantime, Nino wanted to get his brother out of the wreck. He put his fingers into the frame of the door, and the officer later told us Nino curled the metal framing of the door about four inches. He realized he still couldn't get to his brother and yelled, "Guiseppe! Guiseppe! Guiseppe!" to see if there was any sign of life in him. There was no response.

Nino prayed. "Lord Jesus, give me the strength of

Samson!" He went over to the passenger door and literally peeled the door right back. The officer told me Nino ripped the door open. He managed to turn off the engine, pick his brother up, and run with him away from the vehicle in case it blew. As he ran, he was calling the spirit of life back into his brother. Guiseppe came back to life as his brother pulled him out and whispered to him to make sure to get the insurance information.

An ambulance rushed Guiseppe to the hospital, and their friend called the party where they had just come from. All the college guys rushed over to the emergency room to see if Guiseppe was going to be okay.

Somehow, the story of the accident hit church prayer lines, but unfortunately, the story that went out was that Guiseppe and Nino were both dead. This was to be very significant in 2004 when the guys really died because no one believed it to be true, which made it doubly hard to deal with.

When I arrived at the hospital, I found Nino throwing up into a trashcan. He remembered the prophecy from when he was eleven years old, where he watched those men pray for his brother. Nino was badly shaken because this was the very scene he had heard prophesied, and it happened right before his eyes. He had wrestled with this dream many times, and now it had finally happened. Again, my firstborn was declared dead and God raised him up. Our miracle boy, Guiseppe, had yet another story to tell.

The doctors came in and told us Guiseppe needed to be taken into surgery straight away, but Guiseppe would have none of it.

"Mom, Dad, tell them I don't need surgery. Tell them to wait. You bring those college students in here right away." He wanted to use this situation for God's glory. "Mom, you know this isn't about me. We only have a small window here. Please bring them in one at a time so I can speak to them."

He witnessed to each football player from the party, one by one, and they all got saved that night. **That's my God!**

The next morning, Guiseppe was walking with a cane, but his friends carried him to the bleachers next to the football line. They were all so happy to see he was alive. It was a great moment for Guiseppe—seeing all the love and support he had from the guys.

He suffered from his injuries for about two months after the accident. His knee was very badly damaged and he had swelling of the brain, which resulted in massive headaches. The impact of the crash had caused his head to be pushed down hard against the steering wheel and his entire head was full of windshield glass. But my son was alive!

CHAPTER 11

Reaching the World for Jesus

Butch loved children. He carried Band-Aids specially decorated for girls and boys in his back pockets. If ever he saw a
child was hurt, he placed a Band-Aid on the child and told
them that the real healer is Jesus.

Butch saw Halloween as an amazing opportunity to witness. The world comes to your front door, and you get to
speak to every child that comes up. So every year, Butch
decorated the house with bright white lights, and the kids
were drawn to the safety and warmth of our house.

I will never forget one particular Halloween. Butch always prepared something really special for the kids, and that
year was no different. He prepared three different bowls: one
with silver dollar coins, one with massive candy bars—the
biggest I could find—and the third bowl was filled with little
notes that were all promises from God.

Butch answered the door to a chubby little girl dressed
up in a kitty cat costume—she was just adorable. Her daddy
stood behind her. Butch knelt down to welcome her—he
was amazing like that. He never bent over to children when
he was talking to them. He knelt down to their level.

"Now, honey," he said. "You get to pick one item from each
bowl. From the first bowl you get to pick a $1 coin. From the

second bowl you get to pick a candy bar; and from the third bowl you get to pick a card with a promise on it from the Bible. The dollar will last until you spend it. The candy bar will last until you eat it, but the promise of God is for eternity."

Her little face looked very serious as he explained this.

"Now if there's anything you need to pray about, you remember your way back to this house that's all lit up, okay?"

"Well," she sniffed as tears immediately ran down her cheeks. "Maybe you can pray for my daddy?" She paused. "My mom says she never wants to see his sorry face again."

Butch looked up at her father. The man nodded at Butch to let him know the kitten was right. Butch gently asked him, "Buddy, do you know Jesus?"

"No, but if he's anything like you, I'd like to meet him."

Butch led him to the Lord right there! That's how we did Halloween in the Lombardo house. I know a lot of people refuse to participate in Halloween because it is a pagan holiday. Butch decided to turn that dark day into a day for God's kingdom. We lit our house with white lights and prayed for people to be drawn to the peace of Jesus. Butch thought if the world was going to come knocking on our door, we should use the opportunity to give them Jesus.

As they left, the father of the little girl began yelling to people passing by, "Hey, that man is giving out silver dollars." People started lining up at our door.

Next, two little boys came to the door and my three men lit up at the sight of these brothers. They went through the same bowls as the little girl. Then Nino stepped up; he could see those little boys needed a man in their life and asked if they had a daddy at home. They said no.

"Come knocking on this door any time you have something to sell from school," he said. Less than a week later they were back, selling cookie dough. Nino was twenty years old at the time and excited at the opportunity to bless these two little boys.

"What prize do you want to win by selling the most cookies?" he asked them.

With pure excitement on his face, the oldest brother flipped the paper over and showed Nino the boom box, pointing to and explaining all the features to Nino.

"So how many do you need to sell to get your prize?"

"A hundred dollars worth," came the answer.

Nino wrote the check for $100 and had the greatest smile on his face, knowing these two little boys were about to get the delight of their hearts.

I stood, eyes tearing up, seeing those two brothers jumping up and down in the front hallway. Nino's face lit with excitement knowing he had been God's vessel to bring blessing to these two brothers. The win-win ripple effect was God's way of doing this blessing. It always goes both ways.

At that moment Guiseppe and Butch came up from the basement. "What's going on, boys?"

"Mr. Lombardo, Nino just bought all our cookie dough to finish it for us!" the older brother said.

"How many houses have you gone to?"

"This is our first one," they replied. The two brothers ran off screaming, "Wait till we tell Mom."

"How many containers of cookie dough do you think that might be?" Guiseppe said.

Oh no, the light went on in my head. The freezer. Was there going to be room? Need I say this story can be well attested to because everyone Nino knew got cookie dough for Christmas that year. What a beautiful joy that was.

Months went by. Summer arrived, and there was a knock at the front door. I opened the door to see these same two little boys standing there with a little red wagon. It was about 6:30 in the evening.

The oldest stepped up and said, "Is your husband home?"

"Yes," I said. They had tears in their eyes, and had crossed four lanes of traffic to come to our house with this little red wagon. Their baby sister, about six-and-a-half months old, lay in the wagon.

"Your husband said if I ever needed any prayer to come to this house and ask," the oldest said. "Our mother left us to the babysitter, and our little sister is too hot. We think she's sick."

I ran down to the basement where all the men were.

"The two brothers are back. They brought their sick little sister to be prayed for."

Butch, Nino, and Guiseppe jumped to their feet and ran upstairs. Squatting down to the little boys, they asked what was going on. The little boys started crying hard, each one being held by a big set of arms. Butch reached down and picked up the baby girl, praying and pleading the blood of Jesus over her. There was an immediate reaction. She was wide awake, and we could see the Lord had touched her.

We walked the boys home and stayed with them until their mother got home. We led her to the Lord, and we also left them a small amount of money. It wasn't much, but it was obvious to see they could use whatever we had.

All these blessings came from opening our house on a dark holiday and bringing the light of Jesus to where we live. Being Christ every day to our hometown was our hearts' desire.

The Power of Prayer

My husband and I prayed together every single day and studied the Word together. Butch knew the power of prayer.

One day, three of the guys' buddies who had grown up

around the house came by with someone they had just hired. They owned a local construction company and had just hired a young man fresh out of prison hoping to help him back on his feet. They needed to make a run to the bank around the corner and asked if the young man could stay at the house while they went. My men were on their way home for lunch and close to the house, so I told them that the young man could wait at the table while I finished preparing lunch. As soon as the buddies left and I turned my back on him to finish lunch, the young man took off up the stairs, stole a ring, and ran out the front door. I knew instantly in my spirit that he had taken Guiseppe's sixteenth birthday ring.

Within minutes of the young man running out the door, my men and the buddies arrived at the house. They had seen the young man running down the street and asked what was happening. I had just come down stairs from checking Giuseppe's ring box, where he always kept the prized ring, and told them the young man had stolen Giuseppe's ring. The guys' buddies were so mad they wanted to track the young man down and beat him up. But Butch said, "No. Let's pray God has this young man bring the ring back on his own." Butch knew God had always answered his prayers and that God would tend to the man who stole the ring. The Holy Spirit was on Butch as he led all the guys in a prayer asking God to shake the young man who stole the ring until he brought it back.

For three days the young man's entire body shook. While on job sites, the guys' buddies would tell the young man that Butch had prayed God would shake him until he returned the ring he had stolen. By the third day, the shaking was so violent the young man fell off the roof of a house he was working on. Later that day I heard the front door fly open

and someone go bursting up the stairs. At first I thought it
was Nino, who had a custom of rushing to the bathroom as
soon as he got home, but then realized it was the young man
returning Guiseppe's ring. The prayers of a righteous man
availeth much (see James 5:16). **That's my God!**

Reaching the Gang Members

One day, Nino called me as he was driving by the Kansas-
Missouri state line on his way back from work. He felt the
Holy Spirit telling him to go downtown and witness to the
gangs he had heard about hanging out at a car wash.

"Mama I feel the Lord is leading me to this car wash downtown to witness to the gangs. Would you pray with me?"

I started to pray and heard the Lord say, "Tell Nino, 'Go,
Nino! Go!'"

When he got there, all God told him to do was to wash
his van.

The first person Nino met was Joe, one of the guys who
was there cleaning cars to make money. In true Nino style,
he invited Joe to join him for lunch. Joe said he would like
to go if Nino wouldn't mind waiting until he had finished
washing the car.

So Nino decided to clean out his own vehicle while waiting. As he was reaching for his cup of change on the dash-
board, this huge man named Mike snuck up behind him,
pushed him from behind and said, "Hey!"

"Hey, what's up, buddy?" Nino turned around and asked.

Mike seemed taken aback that Nino was so cool about the
whole thing. "You're not easy to scare, are you?"

"God's got my back," Nino said, unfazed by this guy who
seemed to be looking for trouble.

"Don't say that! What do you mean, 'God's got your

back?' Don't say that!"

"God's got my back, buddy. I mean it."

Mike continued yelling and others started noticing, expecting a huge fight to break out any moment.

"Hey, what do you need? You need some money? Do you want to go to lunch with me?" Nino said.

Mike looked at him as though he was crazy. "Man, I was going to take your money. But yeah, I'd like to go to lunch with you."

"Great, but it'll take a couple of minutes. I'm waiting for someone else. Why don't you jump in while I clean my van?"

When Nino recounted this story to our family, Guiseppe and Butch couldn't believe it because the van was full of Nino's valuable tools. Nino reiterated, "Dad, Guiseppe, God's got my back. He sent me in there."

Nino got a big lecture that he left himself open to be cleaned out and needed to use discernment. We were family, and family is allowed to respond to, "God's got my back," with, "You've got to cover your stuff." Let family share, let them have a voice, don't take offense.

Back to the story.

Mike got into the passenger seat of Nino's car. In the meantime, Joe had finished up with another car and had already parked it. He opened up the passenger door of Nino's car, ready to climb in. And who did he see sitting in the car? Mike! You see, these two men were the heads of opposing gangs and had been fighting each other since the seventh grade. You can imagine the fight that broke out! Everyone in the lot threw down their sponges and towels to witness the gang fight of the year.

Nino ran over and pushed both of them apart. Joe stood about six foot three and weighed 225 pounds, and Mike stood about six foot four and weighed about 250 pounds—estimations as retold to me by Nino. Nino weighed in at 180 pounds and stood just over six feet. When it came to living for God, he had no spirit of fear.

"You stop it now or I'll finish it! I don't want to hurt either one of you!" Nino said. Can you imagine the shock? Who was this white boy threatening to sort out these two powerful gang leaders? When it comes to God, it's not the size of your body that counts; it's the size of your faith (see David and Goliath in 1 Samuel 17). As Philips, Craig, & Dean say in their song "Counting on God," we're in a fight, but not a physical one. Our war is not of this world.

"Get in the car, you two," Nino shouted.

"I'm not getting in the car with him!" Joe yelled back.

"Get in, Mike," Nino said, and Mike did. "Joe, I'll come back for you another time."

To get on the highway, Nino had to pull out and drive around the block, which gave Joe a chance to cool off. When Nino came around the corner, there was Joe, standing in the middle of the road with his arms up to stop the car. "I don't know who you are, but I'm supposed to go to lunch with you."

"Ok, buddy, get in the back," Nino said, and Joe jumped into the car and the three of them drove off.

These two gang leaders were confused and amazed. They could not understand what was different about Nino and why he wasn't afraid of them. Nino embraced 2 Timothy 1:7 (KJV), "For God hath not given us the spirit of fear; but of power, and of love, and of a sound mind."

People were usually very afraid of these two gang leaders and couldn't imagine getting them both in the same vehicle. Nino started telling them about the love of God and how God works. These men were shocked, to say the least.

Nino headed off to a little restaurant called City Diner, the one owned and run by Butch's cousins. Nino had to cross the Kansas-Missouri state line to get there. Now, Nino knew it was illegal to cross a state line with felons in the car, but he didn't know these guys were felons until they started getting nervous at the diner.

Nino and these two men walked into the diner, run by his Italian family. They knew the character of these gang leaders and were astounded to see Nino with them. Nino's cousins offered to give them all lunch on the house because they knew Nino was about his heavenly Father's business. They sat down at a table, and Nino ordered a variety of his favorite dishes and told the guys they could take the extra meals home with them. Nino enjoyed every opportunity to show the abundance of God's love.

After lunch, he offered to take the guys home, but they were very careful not to give out any of their personal information. They refused to give their street address and just had him drop them off at different street corners. The only place Nino could find them was at the car wash.

"I don't know who you are," Mike said, "but pray for me." Nino prayed with Mike and shared the love of God with him. As Mike was about to leave, he turned and picked Nino up and gave him a hug.

Nino later told me, "Mom, he was crying and saying, 'Nino, you've changed my life. I'll never forget you, man.'" My son was so blessed to be able to share the love of Christ. He knew he was called to those others were afraid to approach.

Joe didn't want Nino to drop him anywhere that he could be traced. He wouldn't give Nino a house address, so Nino handed him his phone number and told him he could call anytime if he needed anything. A little while later, Joe called, bawling his eyes out, and gave his life to Christ over the phone. Nino wasn't known for backing away from a challenge. For Nino it was never about the level of danger or the area, it was about where God was calling him. He knew the safest place for him was in the will of his heavenly Father. Because of this mindset, God was able to use him in the most unusual ways and places. God takes you where He can trust you. Nino made plans to meet up with these men, but this incident happened shortly before my men died, so they never got a chance to meet again.

I met these men for the first time at the funeral. They never came into the church but stayed outside at the door. As I walked out of the church, I looked up into these two beautiful faces and immediately asked, "Are you Mike? Are you Joe?" Nino had told me all about them.

"Yes, ma'am," they replied.

I reached up and gave them a huge hug. "Don't ever fight again."

They told me they felt too dirty to come inside, but they wanted to pay their respects to Nino, who had changed their lives forever.

As we were busy speaking, the three caskets were carried out of the church and both of these men cried out, "Nino! Which one is Nino?" As Nino's casket was pointed out to them, they collapsed on their knees, over the casket, and began to weep uncontrollably. My son had pointed the way to Christ and brought peace to these two men.

Stories from Paris

Nino and Guiseppe were used to working and being used in tandem with the guidance of the Holy Spirit. In 2002, at the Tour de France, they were walking through the streets of Paris when they both looked at each other and said, "Did you hear the Holy Spirit just say there's a man on the roof of that building who is about to take his life?" They nodded at each other and then ran up the emergency exit stairs. They described to me how they recognized the quickest roof access because of the work they had done on building structures.

Sure enough, there was a young man running to the edge of the building in order to take his life. Nino and Guiseppe ran as fast as they could to reach him in time. Nino grabbed the young man around his waist and flung himself, with the man, backwards and kept holding on to prevent them both from falling off the edge.

"You must be very valuable to the body of Christ for Satan to try and stop your destiny in Christ Jesus," Nino told him.

"I don't know who you are, mister, but you sure sound like Nino Lombardo from Kansas."

Nino, a little stunned, flipped him over to face him. "I *am* Nino Lombardo. Who are you?"

The man could hardly speak. "I'm the little boy you rescued from being beaten up on the playground when we were kids." He was about six years younger than Nino.

At my sons' funeral, this same young man walked down the aisle with his wife and child to say, "I am alive today because your sons saved my life."

On that same trip, my sons called me to tell me there was a riot breaking out in Paris. I remember Nino saying, "Mom, people are beating on one man, and there's such a large crowd I don't think we can save him." He was calling me from a phone booth in the middle of the city. "Mom, you need to pray right now for the power of the Holy Ghost on us!"

I burst into tongues and then said, "GO NOW! GO NOW! GO NOW!" I don't think I actually realized I was saying "Go!" I mean, what kind of mother would willingly send her sons into a dangerous situation? But sometimes the Spirit of God tells you to do unexpected things. My sons knew this, which is why they always phoned me so I could pray for them. They did not hesitate to respond, and they later told me it was as though God parted the way for them to reach this man by moving people out of their way without a struggle. They made their way through everyone, got the man away from danger, and took him back to his place, which happened to be a bar.

The owner shut down the bar while Nino and Guiseppe cleaned his cuts and bruises. Nino, who spoke French, told the man they would be back in twenty days to check on him. Nino even wrote out a Scripture and an encouraging note for him in French, which the man later had enlarged like a big sign outside his hotel. You see, this man happened to be the owner of a popular hotel where the Tour de France was raced. He was so overwhelmed with the kindness and love shown by my sons that he held a hotel room for them when they returned twenty days later, even though the city was flooded with people and every hotel room was booked.

The Nino Thirty-Second Disarmament Story

This story was told to me by a popular football player who met Nino at a New Year's Eve Party one year. He was at this party where everyone kept saying, "The Lombardos are coming! Nino and Guiseppe are on their way," like there was a real buzz around the place.

The excitement apparently really annoyed the football player. He told me people were so excited and couldn't wait for Nino and Guiseppe to arrive. There were, by the sounds of things, plans that night for the guys to go to a lot of parties.

The man was seriously unimpressed. "I'm thinkin' who do these guys think they are anyway? I'm supposed to be the cool guy here," he told me. "A lot of parties? What is that all about?"

So, the story goes that my guys walk into the room, and everyone was so glad to see them that they cheered, "Nino! Guiseppe!" Nino and Guiseppe could have gone straight to all their friends and greet them, but instead, Nino went directly to the football player who was clearly looking unimpressed with the whole scene. Running up the stairs, Nino, with his beautiful smile and his arms raised in the air, shouted, "Hey, buddy. I don't know you. I'm Nino." Then he gave the guy a huge bear hug.

"Mrs. Lombardo," the football player said. "Nino disarmed me in thirty seconds. I really didn't want to like your son, but after that big hug and looking at his great big smile and heart that loved Jesus big, I wanted to be this guy's best friend."

My sons were invited to numerous New Year's parties that year, and Nino said yes to all of them. He was such a sparky person who loved people and fun, but may sometimes have overlooked the details on how things were going to work out. Guiseppe was holding him accountable to his word to go to all these parties Nino had said they would. They would pop in, connect with their old friends, always try to make some new friends, and move on to the next friend's celebration. It was important to them to be faithful with their friendships, and Nino, well, he just loved people and was the life of the party.

So that night, it was coming up to midnight, and they headed to their final party. As they were walking in, they saw a man in the street beating up a woman. Nino and Guiseppe were known for helping women who were in this situation. Nino did the same friendly arm raise in the air saying, "Hey, buddy," but then catching the man off guard, he brought his arm down, elbow first, on the man and knocked him out cold. Nino then sent the woman on her way in a taxi. Meanwhile, Guiseppe escorted their friends safely to the party in downtown Kansas City. The guys stepped into the last party as though the whole situation was normal because, to them, it was.

Another person who was with my sons that night said to me, "To be with Nino and Guiseppe for one night like that made me feel like I had them my whole life as brothers." People wanted to be with them and be a part of their lives. I know this is because of their passionate pursuit of Christ and their desire to show as many people the love of God as possible. This calling was their life. It kept them motivated.

The "Nino Disarmament" story became something this football player taught to many people after that night at the party. He told people about Nino—how his love for and acceptance of everyone could bring down any walls and barriers they had around their hearts.

That was Nino. Everyone loved him.

Nino and the Cruise Ships

Every January for eight consecutive years, our family went on a cruise—all arranged by Guiseppe. We told our friends and extended family they were welcome to join us, and each year the group got larger. Our last cruise in 2003 was one of those great times!

Butch and I were taking a walk on the top deck of the ship, where we encountered a couple from Mexico. They actually approached us and asked if we were Nino's parents. It wasn't a strange thing for people to come up to us and ask this, so we were kind of used to it. My husband and I smiled and said yes, wondering what Nino had been up to this time.

They told us how he was an angel sent from heaven and spoke their language so wonderfully! Their son, Scott, just loved Nino. They had never met anyone like him before. "He cares so deeply." They explained Nino showed up at their door every morning, asking whether he could take their son around with him and show him the ship. They agreed. They would never try and stop such a beautiful friendship. They cried as they told us this, and at that moment, we ran into Nino. He looked very pleased to see us.

"Mom, Dad, I'm so glad you met this family. Oh, hang on a minute." He looked back where he had come from. "I've got a group of kids back there holding the door for the elderly." Nino was twenty-four years old at the time. He was always gathering kids around him and showing them how to care for others. "Mom, Dad," he continued, "let me introduce you to Scott." We turned to see this wheelchair coming toward us and we knew immediately this must be Scott.

You see, we had been hearing Nino say he had a new friend he would like to introduce to us. He never once told us his friend was in a wheelchair. Nino always looked for the handicapped, people in wheelchairs. He made a point of looking out for them on the cruise ships, and he always knew the best ways to get them around the ship because of the times we had traveled with my brother, Timmy.

Nino always tried to make new friends. He would run up to me and say, "Hey, Mom! If you only had one minute to affect someone's life for Christ, what would you say?" He always looked for new ways to be a light for Christ. Not knowing what to say, I often just made up ridiculous things. Sure enough, Nino would do whatever I said and make it look good. This is what eventually lead to Nino getting the events director on the ship to host an eating contest—that

Nino went on to win.

Each time Nino went on one of these cruise ships, his aim was to meet every single person on board and have an impact on their lives for Christ. He would say, "It's a whole week and there's only 3,300 people on this ship. I should be able to impact them all." He put up posters all over the ship inviting people to hear a word brought by his dad—who was given no warning—in the ship's library. He wrote these notes in all different languages to get as many people to the meeting as possible.

"Dad, would you mind sharing a short word to some of the kids before the party tonight?" he asked Butch.

"Sure, Nino," Butch replied, thinking it would just be a small group of kids. But when we walked to the library that night, it felt like there was an important book signing or something because there was a long line of people coming out the door.

Nino waved for us to come to the front of the line. That was when Butch caught on.

"Oh, Nino, you can't just do this to me," Butch said, as we realized all these people were here to listen to Butch speak. He protested he didn't speak all the languages Nino had advertised in. Nino was so excited his dad was giving the word and that he would be the interpreter. Many were touched, a couple were saved. It completely stretched Butch by taking him out of his box; that's what Nino and I were given to him for. Nino was in his element and so delighted to be used by our Father, God. People continually came up to us throughout the rest of the cruise with their needs so we could pray for them. Praise God, we got to be used for His glory!

CHAPTER 12

The Barn

Nino and Guiseppe always invited people over for dinner.
Pretty soon, there were more and more people asking if they
could come. Every night of the week we had several people
come for dinner. Butch decided it was too much, and we
declared Monday night the night for the house to be open. I
started making complete meals for all the family and friends
that would come.

Missionaries and strangers would come to the front door
and ask, "Is this the house that makes dinner for people on
Monday nights?"

We always welcomed them in. Every night after dinner
Butch would get out the Bible and say, "Ok, guys, we fed
our bodies, now let's feed our souls."

One Monday night, we had about fifty people gathered in
the house for Bible study and dinner. I heard sounds coming from upstairs where Nino was busy helping a man get
cleaned up. Nino got this man showered, cut his hair, and
even cleaned his fingernails. I heard him talking to this man
as he worked.

"Hey buddy, here's a toothbrush. Brush your teeth. We're
going to get you cleaned up so you can meet all my girlfriends." Nino talked to him about how his girlfriends were

coming that night, and how he had bought one a ruby-red tube of lipstick.

"You sure liked to brag about your girlfriends."

Nino just said, "Wait till you see 'em. They all know I love 'em!

"Mom, can you get me a trash bag?" he shouted down to me. So I did. I knew it was to fill with this man's old clothes. I waited a few minutes, then Nino passed it back out to me. He had picked out some of his new clothes for this man, as well as some brand new shoes. When Nino did a cleanup job, he was thorough and wanted his new friend to feel like new.

"Hey, everyone," Nino announced as the two descended the stairs. "This is my buddy Ed. And Ed," he said proudly, "these are my girlfriends." He introduced Ed to all the widows Nino brought along to Monday nights to make sure they got a night out and could be around the love of a family.

Of all the people in the house that night, not one of them knew Ed was homeless. Nino and Ed talked that night about how Ed wanted to own his own business one day, running a hot dog stand in Kansas City. Nino asked him if he knew what that would cost and he did. Ed said he knew a guy selling his stand for $1,500. That night Ed left with money in his pocket—Nino made sure of it. The only terms were that Ed had to feed the homeless, but only after they did some kind of work, take care of widows, and help someone else get their "hot dog stand" after he got rolling.

A little while after my men died, I noticed envelopes of cash being left on my table. I asked the girls living in the house if they knew where the money was coming from, but no one did. One day when I was in the house praying, I heard the back door open. I ran downstairs and saw Ed leaving an envelope of cash on my table.

"Ed! What are you doing?" I asked.

"Nino took care of the widows. You're my widow now."

I taught my sons the truth of James 1:27 that says, "Pure religion and undefiled before God and the Father is this, to visit the fatherless and widows in their affliction, *and* to keep himself unspotted from the world." Nino and Guiseppe reached out to widows and orphans while they were on this earth. They sought them out and found ways to bless them and make sure they had what they needed. Nino taught Ed to do the same, and I think Nino would be proud that his buddy reached out to me—now Ed's widow.

Sower's Field

In 1999 Butch began having dreams and visions about starting a Bible college. He thought there were already enough Bible colleges, but people kept asking him to teach what he was teaching on Monday nights. To us, it was just family dinner time. Butch didn't want the label of pastor or the responsibility of a college. He didn't realize that the ministry had already started in our dining room! People were staying at our house until two in the morning because they didn't want to stop learning.

Butch told everyone he was going to build a garage behind the house. Then a man from Africa came into town one day and showed up at our house. He told Butch he knew about the garage and that Butch was "watering it down." He said he knew about the language books and that the garage was going to be a Bible college. That very day we had received a bunch of language books from a man Nino had witnessed to and recently passed away. Butch was not excited, but he began to put together a list of the teachers he knew God was calling to teach in the garage.

My men put so much thought into every aspect of the building. Every stud and piece of wood in the walls has Scripture written on it. Every inch of the floor was prayed over. The guys even vaulted the roof so they could play basketball inside. In 2002, the Sower's Field Bible College officially opened in our barn. It was a two-year course that went nearly every night of the week until the men's exit in 2004. We were only two weeks shy of the first graduating class when the accident happened.

On Friday nights we invited young people over and used the barn for dance parties. We taught young people how to swing dance and young women how to cook. Many people have come and fellowshipped in the barn since then. Today it is affectionately known as the Barn and we still hold classes on Monday nights at 7:00 p.m.

Chapter 13

Butch and Lessons in Marriage

My husband was a gentle man who loved deeply. He was a father to the fatherless. He couldn't stand to see a baby hurt or in danger. If the weather was bad, he would pack the car with a hot thermos of coffee and one with hot chocolate and loads of blankets. Every time we went out in winter, we ended up rescuing someone. There were times when he found families spun out on the side of the road and stuck in the cold. We would wrap them up in blankets and put them in the car with us.

One winter night when we had one of the girls with us, Butch started preparing the van with the emergency supplies. He had the boys get blankets and asked me to make thermoses of coffee and hot chocolate. Butch told the young girl to bring her snow boots. He said there was going to be a storm that night, and if we saw anyone in need, we would stop and help. Because she didn't like the way the rubber snow boots looked, she decided not to bring them so she would not have to wear them.

That night we saw three cars with families spun out on the side of the road. Butch and the boys hopped out and helped the families into our van where the young girl and I ministered to them with the blankets and warm drinks. That young girl with us cried and repented for not bringing her snow boots. She wanted so badly to go out with the guys and help. That girl stayed with us for another couple of weeks, and every day she packed her snow boots in the car, prepared to help those in need—even though the weather was sunny the rest of her trip.

Butch certainly duplicated himself—his loving character and his tenderness—in his two sons. How many men do you know who would take their young boys to an abortion march? "Son," he said, "I'm sure if it was a choice when I was born, I would be dead." What a profound impact this had on the boys and the value they then placed on human life. In my husband's quiet way, he was a strong leader, fighting for those who could not fight for themselves and teaching the men around him, including our sons, to do the same.

He was a quiet man who did not talk endlessly, but when he spoke, everyone listened. His words had weight. He changed the temperature in the room when he walked in. He felt the weight of the gospel on his shoulders and was never satisfied with idle chitchat. In the evenings, he headed to the basement to study the Word of God. He studied so he would always be growing in understanding as it says in Proverbs 2:1-5 (KJV), "My son, if thou wilt receive my words, and hide my commandments with thee; So that thou incline thine ear unto wisdom, *and* apply thine heart to understanding; Yea, if thou criest after knowledge, *and* liftest up thy voice for understanding. If thou seekest her as silver, and searchest for her as *for* hid treasures. Then shalt thou understand the fear of the LORD, and find the knowledge of God." He devoured the Word as one who would seek to show himself approved and always have a seasoned word on his lips.

I always had a stream of young girls in and out of the

house who were part of our family. These were girls the Lord had me raise up and mentor. They would see Butch go to the basement and knew what that meant. They would say, "Mister, don't you know enough yet?" (They never called him Butch. They called him Mister out of respect.) His answer to them was "Girls, you never come to the end of the knowledge and wisdom of the gospel. No, I don't know enough."

He pursued truth like no man I have known. As he spent time with the Lord and in His Word, the Lord would fill him with strength, revelation, wisdom, and grace to pour back into our lives and the lives of the young men he was raising up. My husband was velvet and steel—a new breed of man that God raised up—a man after God's own heart who saw opportunities every day to build God's kingdom and stand strong for what is right. He, in turn, was raising up a new breed of godly men to walk in integrity and be kings on this earth.

Butch, the Husband

Butch knew before we were married that I could never have children. Yet when I was twenty and attending Bible college I became pregnant with my first son. When I was twenty-one, Nino, my second son, came along—yet another miracle the doctors could not explain.

Then came the events of 2004. When I first realized something was wrong and I felt so ill, I didn't want to burden Butch, so I tried to keep it from him and trust the Lord for healing. But both he and the boys knew me so well. There was no keeping secrets from them—they knew straight away something was horribly wrong.

Doctors informed me and my men I was dying. My stomach had become infected with the H Pylori bacteria, which resulted in a lot of pain and discomfort. By the time I went to the doctor it had already developed into 99 percent stomach cancer. All the doctors could say was, "It's over. There is nothing we can do." I got to the place where nothing was going in and nothing was coming out. The doctors said Butch should just take me home to die.

Butch was so devoted to me. He often said he simply could not live without me. The memories of his unparalleled dedication and devotion during my sickness are forever burned in my heart. For eight months Butch tirelessly took care of me. When he had to work he made sure the girls were at the house with me and called the house often to check in on me. He would come in the door, drop to his knees, and thank God I was still alive.

Then, in one moment, I was instantly healed. When I was at my worst, God turned it all around. As soon as the doctors said it was all over for me, God supernaturally healed me. **That's my God!**

Butch loved me with all his heart. People often mistook us for newlyweds in public because they could see how much we loved each other. "Hey, baby," he would say. "I got a crush on you."

There have been so many men, young and old, who have called me, emailed me, and visited me since Butch passed away to tell me what an inspiration Butch was to them, not only as a man of strength and integrity, but specifically as a husband. They all said they learned so much from him by the way Butch treated me in public. Butch modeled or demonstrated to these precious men what a godly husband looks like and how to stay in love with their wives.

One of these ways was through dance, and oh, how we could dance! He always opened doors for me and treated me as royalty wherever we went, like any gentleman should. He protected me and took care of me. Should a situation arise where he felt I was exposed or vulnerable in any way, he quickly guarded me. This behavior is godly covering, how God has designed every husband to cover his wife. If we were in a restaurant, Butch would seat himself with his back against the wall so he could be in full view of the room to make sure he was in control.

"Husbands, love your wives, just as Christ also loved the church and gave Himself for her, that He might sanctify and cleanse her with the washing of water by the word, that He might present her to Himself a glorious church, not having spot or wrinkle or any such thing, but that she should be holy and without blemish" (Eph. 5:25-27).

At times, my husband was creative and spontaneous, too. He bought me the most unusual gifts. There was definitely never a dull moment with him when it came to gifts. They would always be for a purpose, and most often involved spending quality time together as a family or with friends.

One Christmas morning, he woke me up with a huge grin and said, "Babe, guess where we're going and how many want to go with us?" He presented me with a beautiful ring made out of a solid gold Mexican coin, with thirty-two diamonds on it. We ended up going to Mexico for the holiday with thirty-two other friends and family members who wanted to be with us on our family cruise! Butch sure knew how to make a girl feel special!

Butch and I never took our love for granted. We worked on it every day, just like I did the housework every day or Butch worked in the garden. We saw our hearts like land given to us by God. If we didn't work our land it would become overgrown with weeds. So we made a deal to work our land every day to keep the weeds out. I would wake up in the middle of the night and whisper in his ear, "I am in love with you!" And other times he would say, "I got the biggest crush on you!"

We found that prayer was the one thing that really kept us connected. We couldn't go a single day without praying together. My goodness, I could feel him when he entered a room or a mall or a building. I could spot him anywhere. We were so tuned into the heart and spirit of one another.

One time, I was a guest speaker at a conference. I was in a big ballroom in this hotel and had been speaking for quite a while on raising godly children with love and excellence when all of a sudden out of absolutely nowhere, I gasped out loud. I put my hand over my heart, got all teary-eyed and said, "Ladies, I just felt my husband enter the building." They all saw it happen and were completely flabbergasted that someone could be that tuned in to their mate. Butch stuck his head round a pillar and signaled, "Shhhhh!" He never wanted the attention, but somehow, being married to me, we kind of drew attention wherever we went. I believe it was the love of God in us that drew all the attention.

Butch was amazed for years at how this always happened to me—that I would literally feel his presence before I saw him—until the day it happened to him as well.

He was on a job site, busy talking to some engineers and a foreman about a huge government job they were working on. I snuck into the far corner behind him, but when I saw he was busy talking, I didn't want him to see me and break his flow. Much to my surprise, he put his hand up to halt the conversation. He covered his heart and said, "Gentlemen, I just felt my wife enter the building. Would you hold on for one moment, please?" He turned around, and I could see a tear running down his cheek. "There she is. Please excuse me, I will be right back."

He was so emotional he grabbed me and held me tight. It was the first time he felt it, the feeling I had been describing to him for years. We had been praying for it. This feeling is how I think it is supposed to be with Christ. He wants you to feel His presence, just like this.

The Day I Set My Feet Against My Man

It was a spring morning in 2002, and all the guys were getting ready for work. As they stepped out of the door, Butch made an unkind statement. I looked at him with big eyes as tears began to well up. He walked out the door without saying anything. My sons looked at me, and they walked out the back door as well.

All day I thought, I want him to know how I feel. All day I kept thinking I was going to let him know how he hurt me. What he said really hurt and I wanted him to hurt, too.

The problem was, for twenty-five years I had practiced a way of thinking to guard against receiving an offense from my husband. I so adored him. I cherished him and prayed over him every day. I would ask God for protection over him and his job. But not this day. This day was the day I set my feet against my man.

I was stubborn, and for that whole day I chose to ponder on how hurt I was. I wouldn't let him come through the door without knowing I was mad! I planned the whole thing in my head. I had counseled women who knew how to give bad or dirty looks, so I thought to myself, When he comes through that door, I am going to let him know I am mad.

I was in the kitchen when he came in through the back door. The table was all set; the worship music was on; the food was in the oven, and I stood at the sink with an apron on. When he came in, I turned around to give him a dirty look. The look was to tell him just how badly he had hurt me and for him to feel some hurt in return. He came in with a quick thrust in his step across the room, and when I turned to give him the look, I couldn't. I turned back around. I tried again, but I couldn't. I loved him too much to hurt him.

He swept me up in his arms. He grabbed my hand and put it over his heart, his other arm holding me tightly. I dropped my head in shame because for the first time in twenty-five years of marriage I realized I hadn't prayed over him that day. If that had been the day he died, I never would have been able to live with that feeling. I was so in love with him. In the same way people practice doing various things, I practiced loving him. I told him I was sorry, and he lifted my chin and said, "Are you for real? Honey, I am sorry. Will you forgive me?"

"Honey, it's me. I haven't prayed over you all day."

I had planned to break his heart with a look—just a look. My husband was not in the habit of saying unkind things to me. My sons were standing with their arms crossed, watching this moment of forgiveness. We were an open family. They stood observing how to heal hurt. Their father had his arms around me, with my hand over his heart. Our sons watched us forgive each other and hold onto each other. They also watched us go upstairs, get on our knees, and say to God, "We are so sorry we have grieved Your heart today, Father." We always ended anything that separated us with a love covenant. We shut the door and renewed our love to each other so the enemy would have no open doors.

"I love them that love me; and those that seek me early shall find me" (Proverbs 8:17 KJV).

Kiss the Ground He Walks On

One Friday, a group of young women from Oral Roberts University asked me to come and speak in their auditorium. I told them no. I didn't want these girls to get a false image of what I loved. They wanted me to speak on being a woman of God, and I said I would on the condition that they come and meet me at my home. They came on a bus—all twenty-five girls marching into my house one at a time. I told them all to pick up an apron and get ready for their lesson. I had chicken thawing. I told them to get the table ready, that they were going to get the home ready for my husband and sons.

Looking back, I realize it would have been rather funny for these women to come to my house to sit under my teaching, and then have the woman they came to learn from have you set the table and cook the dinner!

That night, the lesson I was teaching was chicken parmesan, steamed broccoli, homemade bread, salad, and all the extra trimmings (sliced lemon, garlic mashed potatoes, and glazed carrots). As I showed them how to prepare and thaw a chicken, I heard the disapproving squeals of all the young women. I told them of the things of God while we were cooking. I also talked about my life and marriage. I taught on Proverbs 9 that speaks of Wisdom and her seven pillars. I spoke for two hours, and at the end I told them that it was very nice having them. They were in complete delight with what they had done and were proud to be wearing the aprons they had at first scorned.

They had become attached to my kitchen. One said, "Mrs. Lombardo, I'm getting married in January. Could you give me one piece of advice?"

"Yes, I would love to. It's really simple. Kiss the ground he walks on." Oh, the sounds of shock and disdain I heard!

They were not at all happy to hear this. I taught them that love loves perfectly. On your marriage day you need to understand the vow you make means you must lay down your life and show Christ-like love every day. It doesn't matter whether he tells you he loves you or not. You tell him you love him. I always told my husband I loved him. In the beginning of our marriage when I told him that, he would look at me and ask, "What do you want?" I answered, "Nothing, dear, I just can't help myself. I am so in love with you."

I continued to tell these girls what it meant to die to yourself and when you chose to do so, you would rise up stronger. I looked at the girl who was making disgusting noises and said, "Alright, Little Miss Attitude, let's do it your way. Let's say your husband comes through the door at night, and he has a headache. He carried the weight of the world on his shoulders that day. But you're also tired and have a headache, and you want him to get you something to drink. You're angry and you're taking all of your emotions out on him. Instead of trying to be a team, you have decided to make everything about you. With this attitude you will only end up getting a divorce decree."

At that moment I heard the garage door open. I realized there were no vehicles in the driveway to let my husband know we had company. He got off work early on Fridays. He came in the house and was on his way upstairs when I said, "Hold on, ladies."

I heard my husband yelling, "Bride of my youth!" which was a favorite quote of his from Song of Solomon. And then I heard him call out, "Is there a woman in the house?"

Other than me, nobody knew this side of my husband. I rushed to the door but it was too late. He had already completely unbuttoned his shirt and opened the door. Then he saw the twenty-five ladies sitting there staring at him. I rushed over to him. "Oh, honey, they will be leaving very quickly. They have to be on the plaza in forty-five minutes." "I'll be downstairs" he said, his face as red as it could be.

I turned back to the young ladies and went on explaining about kissing the ground he walks on and what it meant to honor your husband and die to yourself. Then I heard the door again, and I realized that my sons also didn't know anyone was there, and that it was Friday. They always did something special on Fridays.

They came running up the stairs singing, "We've been looking for ya, because we both adore ya!"

I jumped to run and stop them while the ladies were watching me. The door flung open with two beautiful faces and two dozen roses, both my sons saying, "ta-da!"

I looked at the girls and said, "Kiss the ground he walks on, because one day you will feel so undeserving of the love he pours on you. You will become the mirror of love."

I felt so undeserving of all the work my husband and sons did and all the love they gave, but I understood it was honor's reward.

"Her children arise up and call her blessed; Her husband *also*, and he praises her:"(Proverbs 31:28).

CHAPTER 14

The Exit: Friday, April 16, 2004

"I have to be with you today! I need to be there for Guiseppe's birthday," Kellie, one of the girls who was like a spiritual daughter to us, said to me over the phone.

"No, Kellie, we keep the main dinner just the four of us, and then we open the house for cake and guests later," I said. It was Guiseppe's twenty-sixth birthday.

We had a special way we looked at birthdays. It was never about others and presents, but about giving thanks to God for the life He had given. As parents, this was our time to speak into our sons' lives on the things of God and how they had served Him to this point. We always reminded them there was really only one reason they were here, and that was to point the way to Jesus Christ. They were on this earth to show the love of God to all they would see and meet.

But Kellie was adamant about coming over. In that moment, I felt I should say yes. It was as if something quickened in me. Kellie was a huge part of our lives. Every extended family member knew her. Cherished by all, it was like she was partly ours. Butch was a second daddy to her—he adored her—and the guys were like brothers to her.

So, my day had a guest added to it. It was always pure joy to have Kellie with me. We set out late that morning to shop for the birthday dinner, but it was as though nothing was right in the spirit. I could feel something was very wrong that day. I had this nagging feeling I could not shake off, even though I had Kellie, a real treasure, alongside me.

"Kellie, something is wrong," I said as we walked through the store. "I'm sick to my stomach. I feel like I miss my men so bad, and I cannot understand it."

"Me too! I also feel it." So we both got on our phones and called the guys. They said they felt the same way.

"Hey, how about salmon for my birthday dinner?" Guiseppe said.

"All right. That sounds perfect." We hung up and I called the Mister, the love of my life. I needed to hear his voice. He said he was getting off work early to celebrate the birthday boy.

Kellie and I headed toward home, and as I drove it was as though a weight had been laid on me that got heavier and heavier. I pulled over for us to have lunch, but when we reached the door we both commented on how sick to our stomachs we were, so we went back to the car only to discover I had locked my keys inside. I had never done this before—I was not myself that day.

I called my sister Connie who was only five miles away having a garage sale. I asked her to come over and bring me the spare keys to the car. When she got there, she took one look at me and asked if I was okay. She knew me so well.

"I've never had to bring you keys before, Cindi," she said, concerned.

"I know, something is off inside of me. I don't feel right."

So Connie began praying for me. After she left, Kellie and I went home to unload the food from the store.

After we had set up the kitchen and made preparations for the dinner that night, I told her I needed to get quiet and pray, as I could not stop this feeling inside me. She said she couldn't shake it either. It was around 2:00 in the afternoon when I went to pray, and after about thirty minutes, the phone rang. It was the guys saying they weren't far from home.

About thirty minutes later I took a call from another friend of Guiseppe's. As I was talking to her, Kellie came up and said, "Hey, some state troopers are out front."

"Well, let's go and meet them," I said, not thinking anything was wrong. We took off our aprons, grabbed hands, and headed out the door.

At that moment I was reminded of a vision I had exactly one month prior to the very day, March 16, 2004. As I walked through the door, I realized I was walking through that very same vision right then. Wow, what was happening? I was very aware of everything. There were helicopters over my house. The neighbors had all stopped mowing their lawns and were watching me. The officers got out of two separate vehicles that blocked my driveway. Kellie and I boldly approached them. "Can I help you, officers?" I said.

"Yes, ma'am. Are you the mother of Guiseppe Domiano Michaeli Gial Lombardo the third, otherwise known as Joseph Dominic Michael Lombardo the third?"

"Yes, I am!"

"Are you the mother of Antonino Michaeli Vincento Gial Lombardo, otherwise known as Anthony Michael Vincent Lombardo?"

"Yes!" I replied. My heart was now racing so fast I wondered what was happening. Was this a dream? Was this really happening to me? Kellie and I squeezed each other's hands ever so tight, holding on.

"Are you the wife of Joseph Dominic Michael Lombardo Jr.?"

I could not even let them finish. "Please! Please, tell me! Are they in a hospital? Are they all right? Are they dead? What's happening?"

They removed their hats and bowed their heads in respect. "There are no survivors, ma'am."

Those words shook me to the core of my being. I went down on one knee and Kellie held me. She, too, was in shock, but would not allow herself her own emotions. She was taking care of me.

She helped me into the house, assisted by the officers. I hit the floor and started praying in the Spirit. While I was praying I heard myself singing and realized I was no longer in tongues but in song. I sang three songs in that moment, "Lord Prepare Me," "Purify My Heart," and "Turn Your Eyes Upon Jesus."

When the worst of the worst hits you, the things you have filled up with over the years will pour out. I had filled up with worship and the Word of God, and it was pouring out of me.

As I sang "Turn Your Eyes Upon Jesus," I saw myself lifted out of the house, high in the air, and saw the entire world. The whole world went strangely dim, like the lyrics of the hymn, and then I saw a bright light. All of the sudden, I was back in the house, and my thoughts went to the officers. They were very kind. I was trying so hard to think, but all I could think of in that moment was if the officers were okay. I started showing them pictures on the wall in the living room. "This is a picture of my three men."

I didn't understand the shock on the officer's face or his words when he said, "That's what they looked like?" I did not know until years later that their bodies were unrecognizable from the accident.

I heard them ask, "May we release their names, ma'am?" When I responded with a yes, I had no idea that the helicopters over my house were live news going out all over. I did not realize they were asking if they could release this on the news. I thought they were asking if they could release their names for the official papers. But instead, it went out on the local news:

"Father and two sons die in auto accident on the I-70...they were from Bonner Springs, Kansas. Joseph Lombardo and sons, Guiseppe and Nino were all on their way home...Died this afternoon...More on this later...."

One of the officers then asked me if there was anyone I would like to call? Call! Call? That's when I started to realize this was real. How could I begin to call everyone we knew? I called Connie, who lived less than one mile from my house.

"Connie! Connie! They're dead! They're dead!" I could not stop saying it over and over again. "They're dead, Connie!"

"Cindi, who? Who? Tell me who it is?"

"Connie...Butch, Guiseppe, Nino! They are all *dead!*" I screamed at the top of my ability. My strength was ebbing. All I knew to do at that stage was to call my oldest sister, Sharon, then TK, then Momma, Daddy, and Timmy.

My mother-in-law saw it all on the news before I had a chance to call her. She ran into the street where she lived, screaming and crying. All her neighbors saw her and ran toward her—she was in the middle of the street. I had just managed to get hold of my brother-in-law Mike Lombardo by phone, when the officer at my house came over to me and said, "Ma'am, it is going out on the news right now. If there is someone that should know, tell us."

"Mike! Get to Mom!" He ran out of his place of business and got to my mother-in-law.

I fell to the floor and started crying. In a flash, my heart was made aware of the police officers. I went to them. "Please, may I pray for you? It has to hurt you to deliver such a message." I laid hands on them and asked God to balance their stomach acids. I was worried about them, as I knew it must also have been a shock for them. I made them go to the barn to see what my men had built.

When I got back to the house, I hit the floor, crying, calling out for help from my Lord and Savior. "Oh Holy Spirit, give me strength! You are that same Spirit that raised Christ from the dead, that dwells in me, and you shall quicken my mortal body. You can raise me up from this."

The officer's words "There are no survivors, ma'am..." echoed in my heart for a long time—the words that changed my world in a moment.

Guiseppe Nino Butch

Above: *Taken one month before they passed.*

Right: *Guiseppe and Nino on California's coast.*

Left:
Family picture in Huntington Beach.

Nino, 2 years old, and Guiseppe at 3 1/2 in Easter suits.

Nino making biscuits.

*Nino (in back) believing his muscle was
bigger because his arm was higher.*

Nino, Dara Ann (the little girl from the tent), and Guiseppe.

Top: *Nino started doing this as a little boy and continued doing it around the world.*
Middle: *Nino and Guiseppe in their favorite restaurant in LA.*
Bottom: *Nino and Guiseppe, backpacks on, heading for another adventure.*

Right: Family day at the Liberty Memorial in Kansas City, MO. From left: Timmy, Guiseppe, Nino, Kelly, Mama, Butch.

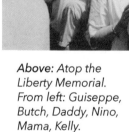

Above: *Atop the Liberty Memorial. From left: Guiseppe, Butch, Daddy, Nino, Mama, Kelly.*

Right: *Nino playing guitar.*

Monday nights in the early days before the barn.

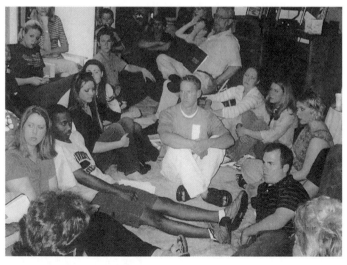

Listening to the Bible being taught on a Monday night in the house.

Worship in the house on a Monday night.

All three guys in the kitchen making a birthday dinner for me.

"WE LOVE YOU MAN"

Above: Butch, Nino, nephew Gabe, Guiseppe.

Above: Niece Melissa with Guiseppe.

Left: Nino, Angel (niece), Guiseppe, April (niece), Timmy (uncle).

Above: Nino, Kelly, and Guiseppe on cruise.

Right: Guiseppe and his grandmama.

Left: Butch and me dining on a cruise ship.

*Me with Oral Roberts as he signs my copy
of his book* The Fourth Man.

*Me in Zimbabwe feeding children in 2007. It was a
privilege and blessing to love on all these babies.*

Butch loving on babies.

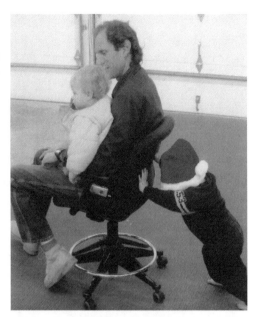

Some of the girls from My Sister's House, in Africa. From left: Anna, Amy, me, Shana, Jaclyn, Colleen.

Above: Sharon (with the bun), TK to the right, me, and Connie in front.

Below: Connie, TK, me, Sharon.

CHAPTER 15

In Memoriam

Butch was first and foremost a family man. He lived for family. It was his greatest passion and ministry. Below is an extract from the obituary the *Kansas City Star*, the local newspaper, published:

On Friday, April 16, 2004, Butch Lombardo entered eternity. He died as he had lived, with his two sons. Butch was a true man. He was a passionate and protective husband to the love of his entire life, Cindi Sue Lombardo. He was a fully devoted father and friend to his sons, Guiseppe D. M. Lombardo III and Nino M. V. Lombardo I, and his daughter Dara Ann DeSoto. He was known as "Uncle Butch" to countless people whom he loved as deeply as any father loves his own children. Butch was a hard worker, an inventor, a general "do-it-yourself" genius who could fix anything. He was an artist and a musician. He was an auto mechanic and a woodworker. He was an herbalist and was great with a sewing machine. There was nothing that Butch could not do. But although his talents were many, his passions were two. Butch loved family, and all that entered his life became family. He was also a passionate follower of Jesus Christ.

While Dara Ann was not a biological daughter, she was and is a huge part of our lives, and we will always consider her our spiritual daughter.

Guiseppe

Even the name of Guiseppe's security company, Command Security, was a testimony to his character. It was the perfect name for his company because he commanded security wherever he went. He had authority, but quiet dignity, just like his father. He brought peace into a room. He made all who saw him feel loved and valuable. He had a magnificent, blazing, passion. He was a scholar, valiant, and chivalrous. He was gallant. His yes was yes and his no was no. If he said it, he meant it, and he would stand by it.

Amy Christine and Shana Nicole, close friends of my sons, both agree that Proverbs 28:1 best described Guiseppe: "The righteous are bold as a lion." When I asked them to describe him to me in their own words, they had this to say:

"Through his words and actions, Guiseppe conducted himself in righteousness, while at the same time inspiring others to greatness through his love. Anytime you were talking to him, you were his focus. You never felt more loved and valued than when Guiseppe wrapped you in a hug. He was constantly a protector to all the young women he was around. He always took it upon himself to guard our hearts by asking us to cover our eyes or turn our heads if something inappropriate was in view."

Guiseppe was a strong, melancholic personality. He was painstakingly detailed and took things very seriously. He also felt things deeply. There was a profoundly deep love in my son that touched countless lives around him.

He was always asking people about their day. He was genuinely interested! He made people feel loved and welcome. He would flip through his phone book knowing there was someone who needed a call. He said there was always someone who needed to hear they were loved and special. He seemed to notice the people who felt unloved and would bring them to the center of attention. Many people have told me Guiseppe made them feel valued when nobody else would have noticed them. He seemed to just have a gift with people.

He was the one that no matter how much time you spent with him, short or long, you felt deeply loved and treasured by him. He had the ability to make every person in a room feel like he was there only with them. He was very tenderhearted, genuine and sincere, but was confident and strong. He would always take a stand for righteousness, regardless of the consequences.

The three of them together were a powerful force. With them you felt safe, loved (actually treasured), and were challenged to live a life greater than your own. They were the most self-sacrificing, but you never heard about what they did for others from their own mouths. What they did was truly to bless others and not for their own gain. They were men of integrity, full of the love of Christ, and powerful strong Men of God. — Anna

He was committed to speaking truth in love. He could make you feel like the most important person in the world. I still remember one of my first times at the house on a Monday night, and he came in and took the time to hug and kiss every person in the room and tell them all that he loved them, and you knew it was genuine. One of my funniest memories is of Guiseppe telling a salesman whom he was speaking to on the phone, 'Love you, bud' before hanging up the call. — Amy Christine

Guiseppe was also a man with presence. He didn't need to speak much, because his presence could say it all. His love was real and uncorrupted. He was a man of valor and integrity. He was committed to doing the right thing. He spent time with the littlest child in the room to the oldest. I remember all those Easters and Fourth of Julys he spent playing with my siblings and me as children. Other people would have rather been with their peers, but that wasn't Guiseppe. He loved righteously, fearlessly, and with no favoritism. — Holly

Guiseppe was a lover. He loved everyone in such a way you felt like it was Jesus loving you through him. His conviction for integrity and righteousness was so strong he would correct you if he felt you were out of line, but it was coupled with such love that you never felt judged by him. He recognized beauty everywhere he went and paid close attention to details, much like Butch. I would also say sincerity is one of the main characteristics Guiseppe showed. Because he was so honest, you never had to wonder if what he was saying was really what he felt. That's partly what made his love so powerful I think, you knew it was true. — Shana Nicole

Lastly, I include how the *Kansas City Star* described my beautiful Guiseppe after he passed:

> Guiseppe was a true man of God, a man of conviction. Many knew the passion of his confrontation but none doubted the depths of his love, for he loved with all of himself. Any who knew Guiseppe knew the power of touch, for hugs, kisses, and pats were a common form of his communication....Most of all, Guiseppe was a passionate witness to Christ. Fully consumed with doing the right thing, often breaking his own heart to either do things right or make them right. Guiseppe loved family unconditionally and prayed for them often.

A poem dedicated to my brother
Written by Nino Lombardo to his brother Guiseppe Lombardo, July 25, 2000.

We've been together through years.
We've spent a lot of joy and tears.
And through the years and tears and joy,
Developed a godly mature young boy.
From a boy into a man,
Time passed in a lightning span.
Walking in God's will and plan,
Showing a life of integrity,
Always on my right he'll be.
The people countless of whom he touched,

To whom love and compassion was shown so much.
His love that flowed like from a fountain,
He makes me feel just like a mountain.
A mountain of confidence and surety,
Because I know he'll always stand up for me.
And though relationships some time shake,
A brother's bond will never break.
Yeah, it's my brother I'm talking about,
The one I could never live without.
Brothers can fight and mess around,
But if you mess with him you're goin' down!
Other friends will come and go,
But if you're like me you'll definitely know,
Whoever seems to be above,
Will never exceed a brother's love.

Nino

The *Kansas City Star* recorded these words about Nino:

> Nino was life. He had a vibrance and enthusiasm that was matched by none. Anyone in the same room with Nino found it difficult to keep from smiling. He was truly gifted. He was an artist, an anointed worship leader, spoke several languages, and had more great ideas than 20 people could ever accomplish. He was a gifted storyteller and an all around people magnet, with a smile that lit up a room. Nino traveled the world for pleasure but never took a trip without finding someone to talk to about the passion of his life, Jesus Christ.

Others had this to say:

When Nino walked in the room laughter and joy followed. He brought the presence of God with him. He looked for the opportunities to show the love and joy of Christ through every situation. He knew the Holy Spirit so intimately, and just by being with Nino, you felt closer to Him. When he worshiped it was so sincere and genuine; he was not leading people in worship to be in the role of a worship leader, but by his sincere worship he led others to that place of worship before God. Nino loved those that others would dismiss from loving; he would take the time to show them their own value. Nino was physically strong but even more so had a mighty spirit in God. — Anna

Nino was inspired. He was constantly talking about inventions that he wanted to create, ideas that he had, music he had written, languages he was learning. He was passionate about life and that passion was contagious. — Amy Christine

Nino had a zest for life. He lived passionately and was constantly pushing the limits. He thought outside the box and never put limits on himself or God. He was so driven and talented, but he used all of his drive to benefit the Gospel and all of his talents to glorify his God. — Holly

Nino was so much fun! Everyone always wanted to be around him! He encompassed the joy of the Lord. He showed that living a righteous life didn't have to be boring. He was so talented in so many areas: dancing, singing, instruments, language, and especially with people! He wanted to maximize his abilities for God; well he pretty much was amazing at anything he would try, which made people open up to him and receive from him easier than maybe going to church. He was great at so much, but never ever gave off the air that he was better. He was excellent in making people feel valued and treasured. — Shana Nicole

I include one of Nino's poems. One he wrote while he was in Bible college:

The Downward Spiral of Sinful Man
by Nino Lombardo

The downward spiral of sinful man,
In the mind is where it all began.
Entertaining a thought you hoped no one could see,
"It won't hurt," you thought, "no one knows it but me."
Down it falls with all the speed of lust,
Bouncing and bumping, kicking up sinful dust.
Until in the heart it has fallen in place,
Growing and consuming all of the space.
Your heart fully captured and chained by desire,
Deep down inside starts an explosive fire.
It blows out of your heart, leaving a terrible hole,
Then spreads through your body, out of control.
Acting on impulse your body is thrust,
Confused but convinced to do what it must.
Destroying and defiling with worldly reason in hand,
You have fully given in to your sinful man.

CHAPTER 16

Mourning

The next several days are a bit hazy for me. There were people coming from every direction around the country and the world. They were trying to comfort me. The funeral was held three days after they died.

All of the local media came to the house. They wanted interviews, but the people close to me kept pushing the media away, trying to protect me. As soon as I heard, I told them not to push the media away. "This is our chance to tell them something positive, to talk about our God on national news. Don't let them come in all at once, just one at a time."

During every interview they asked if I was mad at God because all of my men died at once. I was not mad at God! God good, devil bad, nothing more. He was my refuge, and I knew He was the one thing that would never change. I told the reporters, "You see, I have a great big God who loves me very much. My situation changed, my God didn't."

There were moments and statements God had given me, as well as pictures He would have me see, to use during these interviews, like hearing audibly, "Their very last breath on earth was their first breath there." I saw my men exhaling on earth, and inhaling in heaven. I wept at the revelation that they had no pain. The Father removed them before their earthly bodies experienced anything; their spirits had been removed. The first reporter that came in asked me about the barn as I was walking him through it.

I asked him to hold off from recording for a minute so I could get my composure. I began to sing "Purify My Heart," because I wanted to make sure whatever I said would bring glory to God. I explained to him that sometimes I just have to sing the Word of God to help get the focus off my pain and onto the Lord.

I showed all the media around the barn. They cried, they wept, and they didn't want to leave. I invited them to stay. They held me and cried, and I didn't even know these people. One lady and young man called me the "singing widow" because they heard me singing on TV.

Within one month after the accident I was asked to speak at the funeral of a lady that Butch had led to Christ while picking up a check one day. She said no one ever told her about Christ like he did, and because she knew she was going to die, she told her family to ask me to speak at her funeral. It was my first time ever speaking at a funeral, and I was still trying to figure out how to function with my men gone. The woman's family had no knowledge of Jesus Christ. I spoke to them gently. "Your mother is no longer here. Just like my men are no longer here. The difference is that I know I will be with them again. Would you like to be with your mother again?" With tears streaming down their faces they all said yes and accepted Jesus Christ as Lord and Savior. **That's my God!**

A few weeks later, I was asked to speak at a church on Mother's Day. I couldn't imagine what people wanted to hear from me. What would I have to say? I was no longer a mother! Several people asked me to speak at funerals while I was still grieving myself. I was also asked to be at the baptism of a young Muslim man who my boys had helped lead to the Lord. As I sat at the baptism, the pastor saw me and asked me to come up and give a word. To this day I do not know what I said, but I remember everyone weeping as the Holy Spirit did His mighty work. I still wasn't sure what people wanted from me, but in my heart, God was telling me, "I am speaking, are you listening?"

When the holidays came I was terrified. I didn't want to be alone. I was hiding in a store at the mall when *It's a Wonderful Life* came on the TV. I broke down and asked God to send someone to help me. A youth pastor I had met previously saw me and came to sit with me. He listened patiently and comforted me. He and his family were a kiss from God at the exact moment I needed it.

Why didn't you take me?

I knew my men's last breath on earth was their first breath in heaven.

"But what about me, God? Please take me, too," I pleaded. What do I have to offer anyone at this point? I thought.

I began to walk at night. Several of the young men who knew my sons would come and walk with me for comfort and protection. I couldn't sleep so I walked and prayed and sang songs. I walked the streets of Bonner Springs, Kansas, at all hours. I didn't want people around me. In fact, I was trying to avoid people because I didn't want to say or do anything that would bring dishonor to God in my time of pain. I would tell people, "Don't come around me unless you have a word from the Lord or you have been reading Scripture."

One young man who walked with me said, "Last night I read Romans." As we walked, I gave him the entire breakdown on the book of Romans. Another young man walked with me and said, "I just read Obadiah."

"Obadiah? Who reads Obadiah?"

"Lady, you're intense!"

It was at this time I realized that since God left me here, He had a purpose, and now I had to figure out what that purpose was. What would people want to know from a woman whose whole heart was poured out for these three men?

Before long, women came and asked about my marriage and parenting. Youth pastors asked me to speak to their youth groups about raising godly men. I went and spoke everywhere I was asked and ministered to all that came. Lives were being changed all around me, but I could not see it. My heart was still tender, and it was hard for me to feel anything.

I didn't understand at first why God had left me here without my whole family. Over time He revealed to me that if any one of my men had survived I would have pushed them forward in ministry, hiding behind them and faithfully supporting them in any way I could. God was teaching me that His plans for me were greater than I could conceive of on my own.

People's Responses

After the funeral people would come to see me and try to compare their pain with mine: "My cat died, I know how you feel," "My husband left me," "I lost my job...." God showed me there is no comparing pain. He called me to have grace for them. I wanted to walk away, but He required me to stay and hold them, pouring out love on each one. As I was obedient to His word to spill out love, He poured out more and more love in me, causing me to feel again and to heal.

Two weeks after the accident, people came to me and told me to "get over it; it's time to move on." Some people avoided me all together because I reminded them of death. I learned to say "Thank you" over and over again. It was God's grace on me to have that response because I knew that through those comments they really wanted to help but didn't know how. The right response when someone tries to help you is to say, "Thank you."

Death is not something to "get over." There was life here. My men left a legacy. They loved people, and why shouldn't people feel the hurt of the loss? They were always there for me to talk to, and after they died there was nothing for me to talk about anymore. I miss that.

I offer this word of wisdom when speaking with someone who is grieving. It's not about comparing your hurts with others in times like these. A better response is, "I can't begin to know what you're going through. I can't begin to measure the depth of your love for your mate, for the loss of your children." No one can measure that.

Only through time can you walk out and hear a song you and your husband used to dance to and come to a place of joy instead of sadness. I wanted to run away from every mall or store that played songs because it reminded me of my men singing to me or dedicating a song to me as we danced. Over time I was able to hear those songs again, and now it's become a beautiful memory, whereas before it was painful.

CHAPTER 17

Feeling the Call to Go to Israel

Two weeks after the accident I opened up the barn again on Monday nights. The ministry known today as "the Barn" started with a willing heart, an open door, and a widow willing to feed as many as God would send. I cooked and brought the Word just as we had always done as a family. I remember being overwhelmed the first night with all the natural things that were done by my three men. We all had jobs. I cooked and had the place set. We all greeted and made sure everyone was touched and loved. My heart panicked that first night because I did not know how I could physically love on all the people coming each Monday night (usually a couple hundred that first year).

Now it was just me standing there, and I saw all the jobs that needed to be done: tables set up, trash cans set up, etc. I decorated each table with special touches and made dinner for as many as I could. I held on to my tears until everything was over.

The Lord inspired me with words to speak into the girls of our previous Monday night ministry in the areas He showed me they were lacking. I told those staying at the house with me I needed help loving on everyone who came through the door. I didn't want anyone to come through the door and not feel the love my men used to show.

Several people tried to convince me I should close up the barn and try to get on with my life, but I felt I *had* to keep it open so I could love on everyone who came in. I couldn't bear the thought of someone coming through those doors and not feeling the love I knew the Lord had begun to restore in me.

Several months later, a man named John came to the barn for the first time and said he had a word for me. I told him to write it down. That same night, Pastor James, a pastor from Kenya, Nairobi, was visiting and he gave the exact same word as John. It was the same message God had been telling me. The Lord was telling me to stop making dinner and to start feeding spiritual food. Jesus shut down the "soup kitchen" in His day, and He was asking me to do the same. After the feeding of the five thousand, the same group of people traveled to find Jesus, looking for another meal. Jesus perceived their intentions and told them they needed meat and bread that gave everlasting life (see John 6). I had to feed people the Word the same way I used to feed my boys the Word when they were younger.

When I saw certain people come through the doors of the barn, I felt an overwhelming sense of love for them. Some of them knew my men, and it was over them that I felt the most amazing feeling of love that I couldn't begin to put into words. I began to feel the love from the girls who lived in the house with me, but it took time for me to start feeling love and compassion for them again. I loved them, and I knew I loved them, but I couldn't feel it.

It's important that people who have been through a trauma learn they cannot isolate themselves when they are in pain. They need to get out and help other people. The best thing for me was having other people in pain around me. It *made* me pour out in love, in counsel, and in Scriptures. I would give them the Word of God because that was what healed my heart, that and serving. It took time, but for me it was the most healing thing. The more I poured out on them, the more the Lord poured into me.

I never stopped having the Word read out loud to me. I either had it playing on an audio recorder around the clock or someone was reading it to me. Hearing the Word was the only thing that brought healing for me.

I realized I had always had someone around me to show me love. To not have that joy was one of the scariest things ever. I found it physically painful to not feel joy or love. Shana Nicole, one of the girls who stayed with me, began sticking 3x5 cards all around my room. On them she had written Scripture verses about the joy of the Lord. She knew I had done that for my sons when they were younger, and it was a constant reminder I should not only fill up with the Word, but also that I should focus specifically on being filled again with joy.

Four months after the accident, I was upstairs in my bedroom weeping and praying, asking the Lord if there was some place I could go to just worship Him. I was desperate to find a place to worship Him where there was no distraction and where no one would react to me and my sorrow. He showed me a vision of me down on my knees with my face down on a black and white marble floor and white linen curtains across the windows that were blowing in the wind. On the wall there was a big painting of a rabbi blowing a shofar and several other pictures of different rabbis. Suddenly I heard God say, "Get up and go to Israel."

The next minute, I snapped up and saw that the curtains

in my bedroom were blowing as if the windows were open, but they were closed. I ran downstairs and told all the girls and my sister TK that I needed to get on a plane to Israel. They all stared at me because it had been such a struggle for me to go anywhere to that point. I couldn't sit in a car for very long or even go downtown to sit in a restaurant. I just wanted to be home. TK gently informed me that the plane ride would be long. I told her, "I don't care. I don't care. Whatever it is, I have to get to Israel!"

A short time later, I had another vision in which I saw myself being slapped on the face in the streets of Israel. My brother-in-law Michael Woodall was at my home, and he said to me, "I had a vision that you went to Israel and got slapped. You were on the ground in the streets of Israel."

Michael's face grew white and he started trembling. I told him I was supposed to go, that I couldn't deny it after multiple visions confirmed it.

"You can't go. You're going to get slapped!"

"I've been through so much worse than a slap," I said. "It's only a slap."

Elijah

The night before I was to leave for Israel, all the girls and I were in the living room praying. I began weeping and told the girls I needed God to give me an Elijah word. Not some word that will happen twenty years from now, I needed a *right now* word from God. I asked them to keep praying for me while I was in Israel, that I would receive that kind of word from the Lord.

My flight took me to Tel Aviv, and from there I got a taxi to Jerusalem.

"Why are you in Israel?" my taxi driver asked.

"I want to hear God's voice."

"There is no God!" he quickly responded in anger.

"He's the very breath I breathe," I yelled back to him. It was an intense exchange of emotion.

"I am a Holocaust victim," he said. He proceeded to tell me a story about his twin cousins who were tossed in a fire to be killed and how his mom dove into the fire to try to save them. They all died. He then told about being at Auschwitz and angrily exclaimed, "Is that *your* God?"

I prayed for the Lord to help me and then asked the driver if I could sing a song. He nodded, so I started singing "I Cast All My Cares," a song about laying our burdens at God's feet.

Suddenly, the driver pulled the car over to the side of the road in front of the Citadel David and got out. He looked in the window at me and said, "What is the name of your God?"

I got out of the taxi and said to him, "Yeshua."

"Yeshua?...Yeshua?"

"Yes."

"Your God just spoke to me. His presence has filled my car."

I asked him if he wanted to ask Yeshua into his heart, and he did. With tears in his eyes he said, "I have a word from God for you."

I thought, You have been saved for five seconds and *you* have a word from God for me? I looked at him intently.

"Your God commands you to love," he said. "He commands you to love the life that you live!"

This word hit me really hard. I knew God had left me on earth to be obedient and to serve, but I didn't consider I would ever love again.

"You must say, *l'chaim*," he said.

"L'chaim," I whispered.

"No! You must say l'chaim! with your hands up in the air."

I shouted, "L'chaim!" and felt a physical snap inside my body. I knew God had done something inside of me. I asked the driver what it meant, and he explained that when he and the other Holocaust survivors were set free, they all went outside and shook their fists toward Hitler and yelled, "L'chaim! We are alive, you did not take us!" He stood there and wept.

When we reached my destination, the driver got out of the car to get my bags. He asked if he could have my name so he could write me a letter. I told him my name and asked him his. He put his fists in the air and shouted, "I am Elijah!" I grabbed him and started weeping because I knew God had just given me the Elijah word I had been praying for.

A few days later I was sitting across the table from a young man at a restaurant in Israel, explaining I was having very intense visions from the Lord. I would see something happen in a vision and then it would happen around me, over and over again. "There's a man behind you," I told him. "And he's about to slap a woman!"

Sure enough, the man slapped this woman at the table in the restaurant.

Then I told him, "He's gonna come over to our table and ask me a question."

The man walked over to my table, grabbed a chair from the table next to me, and set it down right in front of me. He totally ignored the guy with me, looked straight at me, and asked strongly and pompously, "What about you am I charismatically drawn to?"

"I'm a widow whose whole family died."

"Get up!" he yelled. "Come with me. I now know why God sent me." He took me to another table and said to the people at the table, "She is a widow. Her whole family is dead. That's all I'm here for."

I thought for sure at this point he would slap me.

The people at the table were the leaders of a large ranch outside of Israel that houses only Holocaust survivors. There were two women, both over eighty years old, who were flown into countries where war was happening to help counsel people about the process of grieving the loss of loved ones. That's not by chance; it's by God. As grief counselors, they only worked with the most severe cases. They explained to me what a person would go through emotionally.

I sat down with the women, and they told me that in two weeks I would be somewhere and all of a sudden I would have the desire to get up and *outrun* my body. One of the ladies said, "I encourage you to keep running, keep running, keep running, keep crying, keep running, keep crying, keep running." That day did come.

Later that same day, I was walking around the old city of Jerusalem when, across an open air patio, a large group of rabbis walked right up to me. I thought again that this might be the moment I would get slapped.

"You are a Holocaust victim!" one rabbi said.

"No, no I am not."

"You are a Holocaust victim!"

And again I said, "No, no I am not!"

"Is not that a glow over your head when God removes a whole family at once," said another of the rabbis. "Is not that a glow over your head?"

I fell to my knees, sobbing in the streets of Jerusalem.

That evening Elijah, my taxi driver from Tel Aviv, came back to find me at my hotel. "I know you are having or-dained appointments by God, and I cannot be without you. I will show you Jerusalem."

I excitedly told him some of the things that had happened to me while I'd been there. I told him I would pay him to take me around. He was over seventy years old. He took me to the Red Sea, the Garden of Gethsemane, and Masada.

When I was in the Garden of Gethsemane, a rabbi called me over and said he had a hard word for me. As I stood before him, he put his hand in the air and slapped me with incredible force. I stood for a second and then hit the ground. This was the slap I had seen in my vision, and though I could feel the sting of the blow, I knew this whole meeting was a word from God being illustrated before me. Then the rabbi said, "Come here, kneel down, and put your head on this rock."

I did as I was instructed, and the rabbi locked his fingers together and then put his full weight on my head, pressing me down into the rock. I thought my head was going to burst like a grape.

"Whoever you are, you were being crushed and pressed like your Savior was. This is where your Savior sweat blood." He lifted his hands from my head and walked away.

My next stop was Masada. While there, I saw a group of Americans. I recognized they were Christians, but God told me to go witness to them. I approached them and asked if they were from America.

"Yes, we're from Kentucky."

"God told me to come witness to you."

They all stopped and stared. I asked if they were all saved and they said yes. Then I told them my story about my men.

"Our group from Kentucky comes here every year and prays. This year God told us an American woman would come here and try to witness to us and that the woman would say, 'I know you're Christians, but I'm supposed to witness to you.'"

I knew this didn't make any sense, but it was about

obedience. They were excited and said they had a place to take me. They asked me to meet them at a café in Jerusalem later that night for pizza.

As I was sitting in the café telling this group of American Christians my life story, God suddenly told me to get up from the table. I excused myself and immediately walked back into the kitchen and asked, "Who in here has been asking for Allah?"

A very large Muslim man picked up a huge knife and came right up to me calling me nasty names. I quickly said, "He sent me in here to give you a message." The man stopped everything when I told him, "Jesus Christ is Lord and Savior." He received the Lord into his heart right then and there. I could see it in his face that he was changed. He asked me my name.

"My name's Cindi. I'm out in the café eating with a group of Americans from Kentucky." Then the Lord told me to turn and leave the kitchen, so I did. I went back out to the table with the other Americans and continued telling them my life story.

Out of nowhere, several Muslim men came through the restaurant with whips and began hitting the people I was sitting with. I blurted out, "Mohammed!"

The Muslim man from the kitchen who had just gotten saved ran out from the kitchen and pushed me behind himself. What I didn't know was that the group from Kentucky came to this café every year and prayed for the city, but they were always beaten. They were prepared for it and it didn't scare them away.

Mohammed called off the men that were beating the Christians. The pastors of the group looked at me and asked, "What happened?"

"Cindi, you will be safe here," Mohammed said, and then

went back into the kitchen.

"We have been praying for a breakthrough in this area of the city for the past twenty years," one of the pastors told me. Later that night, I met up again with the group from Kentucky. They had asked me to come and worship with them in another part of the city in old Jerusalem. When I arrived, I noticed exquisite paintings and peaceful music. They told me they believed the building was the upper room where the Last Supper had been held. Before long I joined them in worship and found myself down on my knees in prayer. When I opened my eyes, I saw the floor around me was black and white marble, and all the linen curtains were blowing in the windows. I wept and wept. This was the place God had shown me in my dream, where I could worship Him.

Two weeks after I returned home from Israel, I was sitting at a local restaurant with my spiritual daughter Kellie. As I sat there, I saw a bunch of different girls come in. As I watched them interact, I saw in a vision the body of one of the girls split apart, and I could see demons holding onto her spine and screaming at her, "You're not good enough! You'll never be enough!" All these young women were dressed their best, and yet they did not feel good enough. The demons just kept yelling from the insides of them. They weren't cute enough; they weren't smart enough; they weren't thin enough. I hurt so bad for them. They were being attacked right there in front of me, and I couldn't help them.

It was so loud in my head, and I felt so overwhelmed all I could think of was outrunning my body to leap into heaven and leave this shell behind. I stood up and ran out of the restaurant. I ran to my car, slipped on some tennis shoes, and ran and ran and ran and cried and ran. I thought back to the two women in Israel. They were right. At that moment,

I wanted to outrun my body.

I continue to cry out to God, "Help me, Lord Jesus! Use me, please. Use me that I may speak into young women's lives so they may see the lies and be free."

Love the Life You Live

After returning from Israel, I realized I had become numb to my feelings. I couldn't feel love for others. My humor was gone, my compassion was cold. I realized the word I had received from Elijah "Love the life you live," was the answer for why I couldn't feel love. God was telling me I had to learn to *love* the life I had been given. I thought the love I felt for my family had been put in a package and sealed up, and that it had left with them.

My whole life I had felt my role was to ooze with love for all those around me. I knew God had placed me everywhere I had been so I could love on everyone I came in contact with. Now I had to pray every day for God to show me how to love again. I needed the Holy Spirit to give me grace every time someone was hurting. He had to teach me all over again how to love the life I was living so I could love those around me again.

TK had adopted a puppy. I had never been an animal lover, but the first time I picked up this little puppy of hers, he put a paw on each of my shoulders, like a hug, and I wept! I was very excited, not because of the dog, but because I had finally felt compassion for another living creature. I knew God was answering my prayers. **That's my God!**

CHAPTER 18

The Barn Ministry Continues

My Sister's House started with just one girl.

"Do not despise small beginnings", (based on Zechariah 4:10). I have had that quoted to me many times in the past years, but as I sit to write this, it is jumping out at me.

Our home was always full of people, but from 1994 to the year my men died in 2004, our home was filled with an amazing amount of young women. There were always functions going on in our home—baking cookies, bonfires, pizza night. At first, they came to have dinner with us. Then those of the age to drive, drove to our house for visiting and for game night.

My husband always thought he would be teaching my sons' buddies his car knowledge. But one night he pulled all the vehicles in the garage. Five girls all wanted to learn how to change the oil, change the air filter, check the fluids, rotate tires, change a flat, and change windshield wipers. They wanted to know the basic upkeep on their cars and if somebody they hired was doing it wrong. The house was filling up with girls. They were coming from everywhere, and my husband told me, "You're going to have to teach these girls."

Then one young girl named Kellie asked if I would teach her how to cook my way. She wanted my recipes. I told her

I was not just a product of my mother, but of many women I admired. When I saw an attribute in an older woman I admired, I sought to get near her and learn from her. I would ask myself how they cleaned something or what was a recipe they had cooked. I became a collection of each of them. I learned from each one and it shaped who I am.

Just like our time with the Lord, the closer we get to Him, the more we are like Him (see John 15:5). When God's Word is all we read, we take on His attributes, we become more heartfelt, and we see the Word made real in our daily lives.

Kellie brought her own recipe book to write down the recipes. While I was teaching her, lessons birthed inside of me. I talked to her about what it was like to be a woman of God.

"Why do you think your house is so different than everyone else's?" Kellie asked one night.

"What do you mean our house is different?" I asked. I assumed the whole world lived like we did. I had no idea how extremely different we were. I thought all women understood that sometimes your husband needs you to be quiet. Sometimes he needs a cool glass of water, or some fresh fruit to raise his blood sugar after being out all day—he's exhausted. The Holy Spirit made me sensitive to Butch's heart.

Butch and I had a code when he came home. While standing at the door face to face, I asked, "Are you home yet?"

"No honey, I'm not home yet. Give me some time to wrap up the rest of my work day." Then he went downstairs to finish his work. When he came back up, he yelled, "Honey, I'm home!"

Then we hugged and kissed, talked about the day, and celebrated that he was home.

The Holy Spirit showed me He gave me, as the wife, authority and power in the home to set the atmosphere. To release love and wisdom throughout the house. I asked the Holy Spirit to teach me how to create a spirit of love in the home. The Holy Spirit showed me that when men come home from working in the world, they have been at war. They may have been exposed to cursing, foul jokes, and lying. They may have had their eyes exposed to things they did not want to see. When my men came into the house, I wanted it to be a sanctuary for them—a place of restoration, health and love, a refuge.

I taught Kellie how the Holy Spirit taught me to be a woman of God, how to hear His voice, and how I prepared the house for my husband before he came home from work. Kellie's receptiveness amazed me. She jumped in and helped with everything going on in the house. I'd see her cleaning the stove, and I'd catch her putting away the spices I had just used. I saw her becoming a real blessing to me, and the more she learned about me, the more she blessed me. Oh how I loved my Kellie.

The Holy Spirit taught me how to teach these young women who came to our house to honor and respect "the Mister," Butch. I wanted the young ladies to see that respect so they could emulate that, too. The more you are willing to honor and respect, the more honor and respect you receive.

The more Kellie was with me, she became truly what I wanted as a daughter. I could see the Naomi and Ruth spirit taking place in the house (see Ruth 1:16-17). She never, ever complained about how much work she did; she reflected the love of God to everyone who came into the house. She greeted people as I greeted them at the door. Then a young girl named Jaclyn wanted to be part of the Tuesday nights I spent teaching Kellie how to cook. So then I had two girls to teach.

One night Butch came to me and told me I needed to start teaching them the Word of God. I thought, *What do I have to teach?* I started praying and crying out to God. I felt so responsible for giving these young girls a jump up in life. I felt God telling me to raise up women who would mother and raise up kings, not kids.

The Lord responded in many ways.

He started filling my spirit with words to give these women. He showed me questions I had at certain times in my early years. I asked the Lord for answers. He spoke and showed me what I needed for a marriage that would bless my husband, sons, and me. The Holy Spirit gave me divine insight on how to raise my sons. He gave me wisdom and words of knowledge. Words of wisdom on how to love when it doesn't make sense! All these same things I began to teach the girls.

I also taught on forgiveness. As time went on, many girls came into our home and I would hear one say, "Well, I can't forgive my father." I would hear another say, "I can't love him. He left me when I was little, and I just can't love him."

I would tell them, "I'm asking you to love even when it doesn't make sense. God says that we love everyone. He commands us to love one another as He has loved us. You don't have to like what he did, but you do have to love him" (see 1 John 4:7-8).

More and more girls began to join my family around the table. Then one night as the years went on, a girl named Jodie spoke up. "Hey, can we just buy a house next door and call it 'My Sisters House'? And it would be all of us girls living there helping to raise up women strong in the gospel."

I was so proud of her. My heart was overflowing. I felt so blessed to be able to love on them and speak into their lives.

They were amazing women, each one getting stronger and stronger and helping the others that came through the door. These young ladies helped me prepare for Christmas, helped me prepare dinners for Monday nights, and helped me love on babies that came in the door. There were so many young families bringing in a lot of children. Monday nights got quite large. When the announcement was made that we were building a Bible college, all the girls helped out. They helped cook; they helped paint; they helped lift boards and bring them into the barn.

Some of the girls would stay out in the barn as long as the Mister (Butch) stayed out there working, often until 2:00-3:00 in the morning. If he didn't stop, they weren't going to stop. My sons would be out there working their hearts out with their father, pulling wire, putting in outlets, framing doors. God was bringing together a supernatural family.

I taught everyone why we did what we did as a family, including confronting one another if someone had a bad attitude or was unkind. So we kept clarity and transparency in their lives and ours. Nothing hidden, nothing secret, our whole lives were an open book. These girls saw everything that went on. We told the truth, even if it was humiliating. When we were wrong, we let them know and we humbly repented before them. Anytime we could see that something was off in our lives, we openly spoke it. These girls all say one of their favorite things was when they would hear the Mister say, "We got to take it to the table." That meant something was going on in the house, and we needed to get it straightened out—everybody to the table.

If we went on a road trip to Branson, just four hours away, but we were going to be gone for the weekend, fifteen people jumped in vehicles and followed us. They slept on floors just so we could all be together. Once, we were going down to a park in Branson to ride bikes. About fifteen to twenty people ended up going with us. The names of people could go on and on who sat at the table and listened to me. I love every single one like they're my own. Kellie, Jaclyn, Jodie, Waheeda, Nina, Bridget, Alisha, Alyssa, April, Missy, sisters Angie and Amy, Shana Nicole, Amy Christine, Anna Rachel, Sarah Elizabeth, Kristin.

You see, they never left me. They are right here, as close as my heart. At any time I need any one of them, they come quickly. At any time they need me, I'll go quickly. We have a sister's bond that will never break.

God gave us something very special when He brought us these girls. I pray they go on to be mothers of presidents, kings, men with the heart of God. I pray they become women of greatness, who know who they are and take their platforms around the world, walking out what their call is in Christ. Out of that group of ladies came surgeons, executives, business owners, and mothers. When my husband and sons died, a great deal of these young women moved into the house and would not leave me. Some stayed a year, some stayed four years, some stayed five. Each one remained for the time God called her. I had six of the girls travel out of the country with me. Women strong in the gospel, raising up women strong in the gospel.

Preparing the House

On March 30, 2004, less than a month before the men died, Nino came home from work very excited. "Hey, Mom, we [he, Guiseppe, and Butch] saw a TV show called *Extreme Home Makeover*. It inspired us to do some remodeling. How about we redo the front bathroom?"

"Does it need redone?" I asked.

"No, we want to do it just because we can. We calculated the hours and it will take us three days. You get to time us." He was trying to make me feel special.

"Do I get to pick out anything?"

"Mom, you get to time us. We get to surprise you. But we have to wait till April 18 because all the family will be coming in for Grandmommy's eightieth birthday," he said. They died two days before then.

After the accident, a man came up to me and said, "I feel I should redo your bathroom. I can do it in three days. The Lord told me to."

"Can I choose the colors or fittings?" I asked.

"No. I don't know why, but I feel like I should keep it a surprise." That caught my attention. Nino had wanted it to be a surprise.

No one else could have heard the conversation with my husband and sons. He put in two sinks. God knew that this house would be changed into a ministry for girls, and they would love the sink and lighting in the bathroom that was all done as a special gift from God. **That's my God!**

Some of the young ladies that used to gather at the house before the accident stayed around for the following weeks and months and wanted so badly to buy the house next door so they could stay close and help me. They would say, "We'll call it My Sister's House. Women strong in the gospel raising up strong women." I was reminded of Jodie's words and knew that was the beginning of a ministry.

These same young girls asked if they could stay with me and have me continue to raise them up. I began to teach them how to take care of a home. I taught them to clean bathrooms, iron clothes, set the table, and so forth. I always told them to set an extra place at the table in case the Lord would bring someone to be ministered to. One night I told them to set four extra place settings, and sure enough, four extra people came to dinner that night. The girls began to learn to listen to the Holy Spirit speaking to them, even through table place settings.

God showed me I had authority in this area because I had already walked through it. It was now my job to pass on the love I had for my God, my husband, my sons, and my home to these girls. I knew I was not their momma because they all had their own mothers. I was becoming a spiritual mother and they all became my spiritual daughters. I showed them what living with Christ and living the Word looks like outside of the Bible, how to walk it out.

I taught them, "A good woman will put her husband in such a place that he will reach his destiny for God's glory, and when he reaches his destiny in Christ, she has obtained her destiny in Christ." God always has a plan for *both* of them to shine for His glory! If you can speak into women, they can speak into a nation. It's a woman who raises the president of the United States.

My Father's Barn

Men began to prophecy over me that I would be given a gift to begin to speak into young men's lives. I began asking God to give me a word for each of the young men He sent into the barn. I prayed they would receive a blessing one hundredfold and that they would rise up mighty in Him.

It was such a blessing to me when some of them began to become part of the ministry of the Barn. God gave me the name of one of the men from the Bible over each of them. We discussed these men of the Bible, and then they would go study and read about each one until they knew all there was to know about that man. I told them it wasn't just a story to read or a person to know. It was *their* family history, *their* lineage, and it was important to know who they were!

Italy Trip

In late March 2005, I woke up in the house and heard, "I've got to get to Rome! I've got to get to Rome!" I didn't know anyone in Rome. I had no idea why it kept coming to me all night. I had no TV so I wasn't aware at the time that Pope John Paul II was dying. At the same time, Anna was working the night shift when her mother informed her a friend had offered Anna an airline ticket to anywhere in the world. Anna slipped a piece of paper with the boot of Italy drawn on it under my door. She said, "Let's go to the boot!" Kellie and I ended up on a plane headed for Italy, and Anna joined us later.

The pope's funeral and mourning were in process. We watched the only English-speaking television program in our hotel, and it was all about the pope. I felt the Lord telling me, "Don't ever make less of the pope."

I took Kellie for a walk around the Vatican to show her where we had visited previously on a family trip in 2000. Suddenly, someone from the media asked to interview us. We were taken behind all of the military blockades, and we were seen on worldwide television. People back home called me on the international cell phone we had and told us they saw the interview.

The next morning I heard the Lord telling me to be ready for a miracle. I asked the girls with me for a piece of paper on which to write my name and contact information and for a €50 bill. The Lord told me to practice pulling the paper and money quickly out of my pocket, that there was going to be someone who needed it today. I told the girls I needed to get to where there was water. We asked a clerk at the subway ticket counter, and she gave us directions to Ostia Antica.

While Kellie and I were on the subway, I felt the Holy Spirit speaking to me. I began singing "I Cast All My Cares." I noticed a man with a baseball cap sitting next to a woman and told Kellie to turn her camera on. I went and fell at this man's feet. When he looked at me, I asked, "Are you Reverend Martin Lombardo?"

"Oh, God, tell me you're not the widow from Kansas," he said, as he grabbed my face. "We have been hearing about you for two months."

"I am the widow from Kansas," I answered, and broke into tongues and gave him a word I had no knowledge of. Kellie grabbed my arm and told me it was our stop and that we had to get off the subway. I reached into my pocket and grabbed the paper with my name and contact information on it and the €50 and handed it to him. He watched us out the window with tears streaming down his face.

Later that night, when Kellie and I got back to our hotel, the man from the subway was standing out front. He told a story about his secretary. She had worked for him faithfully for seventeen years without pay, and he felt the Lord had told him to honor her and to take her to the most exclusive restaurant for dinner. He only had enough money to pay for the subway ticket that night, and that was it.

He told us the the subway incident from his perspective, that he was telling his secretary how great their dinner was going to be when all of a sudden a woman bows at his feet and tells him things he had been waiting seventeen years to hear from the Lord. He told us that because of the exclusive nature of the restaurant that they had eaten at, the bill with tip was €50! **That's my God!**

He also said he was best friends with Pope John Paul and that for the last seventeen years he was told God was going to give him a word. He wrote the story down and asked me to bring it back to the States and give it to a certain pastor in Kansas. Kellie and I were astonished because we had just started attending that church.

Roses on Friday!

When my sons were growing up they would get me roses on Fridays, one rose most of the time, every now and then a full bouquet. Mostly throughout life, just one rose. When they started their own companies at ages seventeen and nineteen, they brought me full bouquets every Friday.

They wanted to treat me as they would their wives. They wanted to practice on me so it would be natural in marriage. They knew what they worked on beforehand would make their marriages better.

They sent me thank you notes and made up songs. They opened my car door for me, as well as other doors. When they came home from school or work, they checked my car and filled it with gas when needed and then washed it down. Then they'd come in the house and say, "Momma, your car is full with gas and clean." I didn't ask them to do these things, and it was so sweet of them to do them. It was their hearts to serve and love on me.

When they were in their twenties, they made a production of giving me flowers on Friday.

While singing some great song, they would stomp out a beat on the staircase coming in through the garage into the dining room. Sometimes I would laugh and cry all at once. What great men they had grown into.

One time while I was holding a meeting in my house, young ladies had come from Oklahoma to listen to me. They came on a bus that they parked across the street. So to Guiseppe and Nino it looked like we did not have anyone in the house.

I was speaking on pouring yourself out as though you were Christ, "Kiss the ground he walks on!" and raising kings, not kids. My heart was to raise men to let them be all they were called to be, not too emasculate them.

So on this particular day while I was speaking, I heard the garage door go up and realized the men did not know anyone was here. They started their routine they had made for the Friday roses, singing "We been looking for you because we both adore you." As they threw open the back door from the garage, they said, "Happy Friday roses, Momma!"

I was laughing so hard, but they were shocked to find the house full of young women. They kissed me on both sides of my face and apologized for interrupting. I turned to the young ladies who were in awe and said, "Kiss the ground he walks on. It will come back to you more than you can ever imagine."

For five years after the men had exited to heaven, I received roses on Friday. I was in an international airport and a little boy ran up to me, gave me a rose, and said, "Happy Friday, lady." My mouth just dropped open. I was so blessed and missing my family so much as I watched the little boy run away. When I arrived in Africa, little boys ran up to me singing a song they had written for me and gave me roses. Yes, it was Friday. I was in Africa for six weeks and roses came every Friday. When I was at home, roses arrived on Fridays at the house.

One day one of my young ladies mentioned to me that she had noticed roses were coming to me no matter where I was on Fridays. All of the sudden it hit me. They do! They do! They come on Fridays. **That's my God!** He wants me to know my men are always with me; they are only a veil away."

I was in Rome, a man gave me a rose.

I was in Prague, a little boy ran up and gave me a rose.

In France, a man came up, gave me a rose, and left saying nothing. All on Fridays.

Once in the middle of a desert area in Africa, a little boy ran up and gave me a rose. I could not figure out where he could have possibly gotten a rose in such a place, but then, **that's my God!**

When I came home to the US it still happened every week. Roses came on Friday for five years without a break. One night when I was down in Branson, Missouri, staying at my parents' house, Shana Nicole, one of my young ladies that had grown up around the house and in the ministry, came down to be with me. She knew when I woke up in the morning it would be April 16, the memorial day of my men passing away.

After work she drove four hours just to be with me. She spent the night talking to me, only to wake up and be back at work in her own salon by ten in the morning.

That was a sacrificial gift of love. I was so grateful to see her that night. As we talked, laughed, and went through memories, my phone rang and a voice on the other end said, "Is there anyone home at your mom's house? I'm at the front door, and I saw the light on but I didn't want to wake anyone."

I went to the door. There stood a young man named Dominic. "I don't know what this is about, but I felt the Lord say I had to get here and hand you three roses one minute after midnight. Here, these are the three roses. Good night." And he left. He didn't know it was the date of the memorial.

Shana Nicole said, "It's April 16, Pastor Cindi." Then she said with sweet surprise, "Oh my goodness it's Friday roses! They came one minute after midnight, on Friday, three roses for your three men! God had it delivered by Dominic."

Roses still come to this day, though not every week anymore. One young man who knew my sons was heading over to visit me and remembered it was Friday. He only had $1 on him but had heard God tell him to stop and ask for a bouquet of roses and to tell the story to the florist. He stopped at the local grocery store and asked the florist if he could speak with her. He explained he only had a dollar and then told her my story. "Miss, it's Friday and I need a bouquet of roses." She knew who I was and sent him with the roses. He came in smiling and told me what had just happened. **That's my God!**

There are so many stories of God sending roses on Fridays, these are just a select few. You see, God cares about the little things and the big things in our lives. He cares about our hearts. That's God. The bad things that happen are not God. God good! Devil bad! Don't try to go deeper. That is what the devil wants you to do. He wants you to blame the God who cares so much He gave His only Son.

Blessed Assurance

A few months after the men had passed I was praying in the barn, asking God to please send someone to sing "Blessed Assurance" to me. My heart was aching to hear that song sung to me, and I did not know why. The Lord told me, "Get up off the floor. They're coming. Ready yourself."

That night the Lord brought a family from Africa to the barn. A woman and her children got up and sang that song to me. They ministered to me. Her husband, who was a pastor, said he felt the Lord told him to tell me, "You were made for such a time as this, and He is going to raise you up." He asked me to come to Africa.

Six months later, in June 2005, I went to Africa for the first time. It opened the door for other international speaking opportunities.

Chapter 19

Divine Romance

I spent ten years as a widow, walking out God's plan, feeling comfortable with who I was, seeing and moving in the gospel, hearing His word. One day, I felt a change coming. But I did not expect *this*.

June 17, 2013, I was in the barn praying and worshiping around 7:00 a.m. I heard the Lord say twice, "I am bringing your husband. Quickly! Quickly! He'll be full of honor, full of the Word of God, ready to walk alongside of you and to love you well." Then God showed me a man who was sent to do nothing but love me well, and I couldn't even figure out what that looked like, but I kept hearing it.

"I love my life with You. I love my life. I don't need to share it with someone else. I don't want to get started down that road," I told the Lord. "I see the importance of me being alone and quickly going, not having to deal with another person's emotions. I've seen other husbands and wives fight and don't want anything to pull against the ministry."

The Lord said again, "I am bringing him quickly. I'm bringing him as an armor bearer." My armor bearers (people called to serve and walk alongside me as they learn in the ministry) and all my girls around me had heard at some time or another in ministry that I was going to marry again, and it would be a much younger man. Over the ten years of ministry after my men had exited, I received countless words from prophets, ministers, and pastors that I would remarry a younger man. None of this took away the shock of what happened later that night.

I then heard the Lord say, "Write a note and stick it under that chair." So I got a marker and a large white sheet of paper and wrote on it, "Welcome home, your burden has been lifted, _____ _____." I left off the last two words, and stuck the note under the chair the Lord directed me to in the barn. The last two words the Lord told me to write were "my husband." I left them off because I was still in shock. I went about my day with a very busy schedule and completely forgot about this event.

At 7:30 that evening, I greeted everyone in the barn for Monday night. I started speaking on the prophetic, on giving a word from God. "Surely the Lord GOD will do nothing, but he revealeth his secret unto his servants the prophets" (Amos 3:7 KJV).

As I was teaching I heard the Lord say, "Tell them to get their phones out."

"Everybody, get your phones out. Put on a ten-minute timer." I repeated this statement a couple of times; it was what I got. It took a few moments for everyone to get their phones out and put on their timers.

I said it as I was hearing it from God.

"Ten-minute timer. God says to tell you in ten minutes a man's going to walk through that door (I pointed to the south door). He's going to be full of honor, full of the Word of God, ready to go as an armor bearer to cover me well, and (I began to mumble) to love me." I repeated the statement a couple of times and went back to teaching on the prophetic.

So I went on talking, giving the message I had planned for that night, and five people came from the north side, two women and three men who sat in the second row.

People were waving their phones at me and showing me their timers.

"Stop it," I said. "Five minutes. Five people. God said *that* door (as I pointed), not that door. Don't try to make something fit. I'm not afraid of being wrong; I'm afraid of disobedience. I'd rather say it and be wrong," shot out of my mouth. I reminded them of what God said. I went through the entire statement so strongly. "Full of the word of God, and he's gonna sit in *that* chair. Watch it." And I gasped as I realized I pointed at the chair I had put the note under. I hadn't told anyone about the note.

Now the new people that had just come in had been filled in and updated on what was going on, that there were timers on to watch God send someone through the south door.

I got back into my message, was going along in the meat of the Word, my mind no longer on the timers but on the message. The timers started going off. And the back row of people were waving their phones and pointing toward the door.

"What? What's going on?" I said.

They were pointing at the south door, then my timer went off, and there stood a man. I said, "Hello, there."

He nodded and said hello as he came in. If you could get what happened inside of me at that moment. When I looked up and saw him in the door, I saw something the size of a softball glowing bright white, coming from him to me. When it hit me, it had a physical sensation to it as if I had swallowed water hard and it was stuck in my chest.

He went to sit in the chair (yes, that chair with the note on it!). I was immediately aware of his age. I just tried to completely ignore him and move in the Word. The Lord had me prophesy over one of the new men who had come in at the five minute mark. I told him what was going on in his life; it was all true. God gave me words for the two women; all true. When I prayed for them they went down in the Spirit and were hit by the Lord. Not until an hour later when I was introduced to them did I learn these were the parents and sister of Neil, the man who came in the door and sat in the chair.

God sent them in early to hear the word released. Neil had been sent earlier than when he entered. He came in his own car and sat in it, praying outside the barn. He was exhausted after a day's work. He'd heard about the lady in the barn and was coming to meet her. When he got out of his car he went to the north door and was going to come in when he heard the Lord say, "No, go to the other door." He walked around and opened the south door at the very moment the timers went off.

God loves me that much that He would do it so exactly. There was a note under the chair, and I didn't even want him to know it because if he knew about it, I would have to tell him. I felt God tell me to take the note into the house and put it on the table—out in the open so everyone could ask about it. God told me to put it out on the table so I would have to point it out every day. I couldn't have someone saying they hadn't seen it.

After two weeks I put the note away.

A month or two later, Neil asked to be part of the ministry.

I already knew God had sent him in. I was trying to walk in obedience, but also be careful and keep my distance. I filled Neil in on what he needed to read. I tried to be discerning and asked myself, "Is this a trick?"

Neil joined the ministry and, while speaking with another armor bearer, learned about the note. From time to time, he asked me, "What was on the note? Was there something more?" I would just stare at him and walk away.

I was asked to speak at a crusade in Kentucky, and Neil was going to armor bear for me. He had heard God say he was to go. I knew if the miracles stopped, Neil was a trick. We saw a woman who had been using a walker, dragging her leg and arm, throw away her walker and dance like a ballerina after we prayed for her. The deaf we prayed for received their hearing. After we returned home from the crusade, the pastor called and told us every barren woman we prayed for had become pregnant.

Just after the crusade, I began preparing to go to Africa. Neil came to me and said, "I believe I'm to pursue you with the intent of marriage. Would you seek God in this matter?"

"No," I said, and walked away.

Before I left for Africa, he came to me at least six times with the same request. He asked God for another sign, another dream, and it kept happening. He said, "Lord I will walk away if you tell me to walk away."

Finally, I said to him, "I understand you've never dated, never kissed a girl. I encourage you to date. I'm leaving the country for six weeks. If you need to leave this ministry, I understand. Move on."

I got on a plane to Africa. The first place I landed, the pastor and his wife told me that three weeks before I got there, the Lord continually told them my last name would change. Secondly, the pastor's wife said, "One year ago the Lord had me start praying for you; that He's bringing your husband, and he's younger than me." She wept and wept for months until the Lord settled her heart with it. Neil is younger than she is.

Another pastor and prophet said to me, "Pastor Cindi, you fear man more than you do God. You're in disobedience." Another pastor said, "God has shown me that He has placed the courage in the heart of one of your armor bearers to ask you to marry him." I began asking people to repeat the words as I recorded them with my phone.

Whenever I was traveling, someone in the ministry would send me text messages to inform me about anything that was going on and if any business needed to be attended to. At this time, Neil was the only one with a working phone, and he was sending the updates. I thought, Sure, great, all I need is more contact with this guy.

I told a pastor in Africa the whole story, and he asked me, "What was left off the note? What did you leave off the note? The Lord keeps waking me in the night telling me something was left off of the note."

At the same time that pastor was asking me the question, Neil texted me. "Pastor Cindi, I need to know what was on the note. What was on the note? What did you leave off?"

The pastor said, "He has to know."

I sent Neil the answer. "Welcome home, your burden has been lifted, MY HUSBAND."

Neil responded, "I knew it!"

Do you know how shocking that was? He kept asking because he knew it had to do with his destiny in Christ. The first night he came to the barn, God gave him a word that I had a key to his destiny in Christ. It was true.

Neil was so elated.

He asked if he could pursue me with the intent of marriage, and I finally said yes.

On the day I told Neil yes, I sent him all the voice recordings of the prophecies spoken by these men and women. It was eight months of my remaining silent, not letting anyone know a thing.

As soon as I said yes to Neil, I asked my mom to move into the house with me and stay with me every night until the wedding so there could be no persecution or any lies about what was going on.

The Holy Spirit opened my heart to fall in love with such a great man.

Neil was always doing things for me that were secret desires in my heart only the Lord knew about. He would leave me love notes with Scriptures on them that the Lord had been speaking to me about privately. The questions I asked God in secret, Neil would send me responses to without knowing. On the one-year anniversary of our meeting, June 17, 2014, Neil gave me a ten-minute timer, and he wrote all these ten-minute things like "If we ever fight, let's set this timer." How much love he poured out on me. He was so creative and still is.

In August, I was coming back to Kansas City from Texas with my mom when I received a phone call from Neil. "Honey, can we have date night tonight?"

"Yes, but I need an hour to get myself ready after we get home." Mom was going to dinner with my sister that night.

Neil came to pick me up. He had been driving around praying, and God showed him where we could watch the sunset. We pulled into Union Station and walked to Liberty Memorial for WWI veterans in downtown Kansas City. I got so excited. "Do you know what this place means to me?"

"Tell me. Why is it so important to you?"

I told him this place was important to my entire family. I was crying and laughing all at once because that is where God brought us to watch the sunset. It was August 2, 2014.

We were so thrilled just being together. I noticed he was texting, and I asked if he was working.

"Yes, just a second." He finished his text and put away his phone as we walked up the beautiful stairs my mom and dad had run up on their very first date. My men had the alarm system contract on it. We had a family picture with Mom and Dad and four of us at the top. I told him all these things as we walked to the top of the Liberty Memorial. Neil and I walked around the base of the tower talking and loving our time together. I noticed the door of the tower was open, and I got excited.

"Oh, Neil, maybe we can go to the top and watch the sunset....No, we'd have to go to the bottom and get a ticket and it will be closed by then."

"Let's try. Let's just go ask the girl standing there," he said.

Little did I know, he had set up a fake conversation with this young girl and had rented the entire Liberty Memorial with its 217 foot tower. So he asked if we could go up, but she said it had been booked for an after-hours party.

"Is it before 'after-hours'?" he asked. I was so excited he was willing to see if we could go up to the top.

She reluctantly agreed and told us not to tell anyone. We only had fifteen minutes. We got in the elevator and I looked at Neil. "We have the favor of God on us!" I giggled with excitement. While we overlooked all of downtown I told him some of Kansas City's history. "Hey, can we make a video for Mom and let her know we're up here?"

"Sure, honey."

It was as if we were on cloud nine having the best time when I realized it had gotten dark. "Oh my gosh, we better go down."

"Wait a minute, sweetie, I left a note for you up here."

"What?"

"I wrote a note for you. Look over the edge."

I looked over. "It looks like my name in lights!" It was my name in thirty-foot letters of lights, with a dot, dot, dot after it.

"Yes, it is, but I left something off."

I turned and saw him on one knee. "Will you marry me?"

"Yes, yes!"

He jumped up, leaned over the edge, and screamed, "She said yes!"

I leaned over and yelled, "Who's down there?"

"People you know," Neil said.

My mom, sisters, and closest friends were all down there and came up to the top with us because it was rented for our party. We were the after-hours event! Momma asked if Neil knew how much this place meant to me. We told her he hadn't known, but God had shown him this was the place he was to propose. **That's my God!** He knows the heart of his daughter!

We were married September 21, 2014.

Looking back a few years before meeting Neil, I remember going for a walk with Dominic Haygood. After he had asked question after question about everything that had happened to me and my family, he turned to me, eyes tearing, and said, "It can't end this way! If God is real, then a handsome prince has to come and carry you off. He would not have such a wonderful family with so much potential and love all at once leave you here without someone to love on you!"

God is real, Dominic!

He sent him.

But Neil came as a king, not as a prince. He took the authority given to him by God in His Word, and he grabbed my heart.

It has been an amazing adventure, full of the deepest love I have experienced in my life, and I have already had a life of great love. I had three men who loved me dearly. I had a husband who loved me big. My sons loved me big. I knew as a woman of God what it was like to have big, precious, deep love every day. But when God brought Neil, it was a greater love than I ever expected. I could not have imagined a greater love, something deeper, something more.

It is a divine love, a divine romance.

Neil's and my first kiss at the altar.

CHAPTER 20

Looking Ahead

As I think of the incredible journey the Lord has brought me on, I am excited to see what He will do in the future. I would love to see a school of excellence established. I'd love to see young people trained to take television and different platforms for Christ. We live in an end-time media blitz! It's like a Super Bowl and we're at the end of the game! It's time people begin to train themselves. The more they prepare themselves, the more God can use them! I want people with degrees. The top of the top, so they can hit the top of the top. I want to see all of my "kids" hit it high! Don't aim low! Don't allow the world to describe you. We all need a man or woman of God to come alongside and say, "Do you know what greatness I see in you?" Elisha got next to Elijah, and Elisha learned. He also received double the anointing. The more you walk with someone who has walked through a lot in life, the more you will learn how to overcome things that come at you.

I would love to have more world travel opened up to me. I'd love to take young people around the world and show them where Christ lived, where history happened in different places. There are so many places in this world that tell the story of Christ. God is still speaking to us!

I want people to learn to walk in their prophetic gifting. They need to be taught what a false prophet looks like so they'll know the difference when they get a real word from God.

I feel like God is teaching me to tell others about how real God is to me so others can believe He will be that real to them as well. The more I share my experiences, the more they realize they've had the same ones. I want people to have an "aha!" moment where they realize, "That was God! **That's my God!**" They will realize nothing happens by chance—it happens by God.

I want people to stop blaming God. Devil bad, God good! People ask me all the time, "Were you mad at God?" I tell them no. He is the One who loved me and held me through the storm. The enemy created the storm. The enemy wants to hit you and hit you when you are down. He is the one trying to get us to speak against God.

I have nothing to say against God. The Lord is the one who wants to lift you up when you are down. I don't want people blaming my God for the enemy's lies or actions. The Lord gave me my husband. He gave me my two sons. He blessed us with an amazing home of love and life. I got to do everything I wanted to do with my family. I traveled the world with them. We opened our home to love on all those we could.

I want people to stop judging and condemning and start loving and raising up. Stop blaming the past and create your future. Determine to leave the past behind you, but learn from it. Don't drag it around with you like a dead weight.

My men are about their Father's business, running the heavenlies. I believe they are up there preparing to come back for the end time war. God is preparing them now to be well trained for what they are called to do. He knows He took warriors!

What I want people to take away from this book is that God is real. He is my God, and He is your God.

He is speaking! Are you listening?

1 Thessalonians 5 (KJV)

[1]But of the times and the seasons, brethren, ye have no need that I write unto you.

[2]For yourselves know perfectly that the day of the Lord so cometh as a thief in the night.

[3]For when they shall say, Peace and safety; then sudden destruction cometh upon them, as travail upon a woman with child; and they shall not escape.

[4]But ye, brethren, are not in darkness, that that day should overtake you as a thief.

[5]Ye are all the children of light, and the children of the day: we are not of the night, nor of darkness.

[6]Therefore let us not sleep, as do others; but let us watch and be sober.

[7]For they that sleep sleep in the night; and they that be drunken are drunken in the night.

[8]But let us, who are of the day, be sober, putting on the breastplate of faith and love; and for an helmet, the hope of salvation.

[9]For God hath not appointed us to wrath, but to obtain salvation by our Lord Jesus Christ,

[10]Who died for us, that, whether we wake or sleep, we should live together with him.

[11]Wherefore comfort yourselves together, and edify one another, even as also ye do.

[12]And we beseech you, brethren, to know them which labour among you, and are over you in the Lord, and admonish you;

[13]And to esteem them very highly in love for their work's sake. And be at peace among yourselves.

[14]Now we exhort you, brethren, warn them that are unruly, comfort the feebleminded, support the weak, be patient toward all men.

[15]See that none render evil for evil unto any man; but ever follow that which is good, both among yourselves, and to all men.

[16]Rejoice evermore.

[17]Pray without ceasing.

[18]In every thing give thanks: for this is the will of God in Christ Jesus concerning you.

[19]Quench not the Spirit.

[20]Despise not prophesyings.

[21]Prove all things; hold fast that which is good.

[22]Abstain from all appearance of evil.

[23]And the very God of peace sanctify you wholly; and I pray God your whole spirit and soul and body be preserved blameless unto the coming of our Lord Jesus Christ.

[24]Faithful is he that calleth you, who also will do it.

[25]Brethren, pray for us.

[26]Greet all the brethren with an holy kiss.

[27]I charge you by the Lord that this epistle be read unto all the holy brethren.

[28]The grace of our Lord Jesus Christ be with you. Amen.

My Life Statements and Verses

I love quoting all the Scriptures out loud to feed my body, soul, and spirit. These three verses and statements were food to my soul and part of what sustained me in my toughest hours. I pray they strengthen you as they strengthened me.

I am the righteousness of God!

For he hath made him to be sin for us, who knew no sin; that we might be made the righteousness of God in him. (2 Corinthians 5:21)

I can, and I will, do all things through Christ Jesus who strengthens me!

I can do all things through Christ which strengtheneth me. (Philippians 4:13)

Greater is He that is in me than he who is in the world!

Ye are of God, little children, and have overcome them: because greater is he that is in you, than he that is in the world. (1 John 4:4)

Appendix

Below are some of the resources God has used to inspire me throughout my life.

Books

The Power of Praise and Worship by Terry Law

Praise Releases Faith by Terry Law

The Truth About Angels by Terry Law

Good Morning Holy Spirit by Benny Hinn

God's Generals: Why They Succeeded and Why Some Failed by Roberts Liardon

The Fourth Dimension by David Yonggi Cho

Battlefield of the Mind by Joyce Meyers

Me and My Big Mouth!: Your Answer Is Right Under Your Nose by Joyce Meyers

What the Bible Says About Child Training by J. Richard Fugate

Apps

EV: Emergency Verse. To quickly reference Bible verses on important topics. Available on the Apple App Store for iPhone and iPad. emergencyverse.com. Neil created this app for me on a road trip so I could quickly find and send biblical answers to the people in our ministry! I love it!

For further information on Cindi Lombardo-Gunsalus and additional resources please visit her websites, pastorcindi.com and myfathersbarn.com.

My Father's Barn
MINISTRIES

Neil and Cindi Lombardo-Gunsalus are the pastors at My Father's Barn in Bonner Springs, Kansas. My Father's Barn is a ministry led by the Holy Spirit and rooted in the Word for the purpose of teaching and equipping the body of believers to live out their calling, while growing in Christ.

The Barn is a place for all to see God's love demonstrated, feel the Holy Spirit's peace, and hear the truth by which we are set free. For more information and resources, please visit: myfathersbarn.com